## ACLS History E-Book Project

Reprint Series

The ACLS History E-Book Project (www.historyebook.org) collaborates with constituent societies of the American Council of Learned Societies, publishers, librarians and historians to create an electronic collection of works of high quality in the field of history. This volume is produced from digital images created for the Project by the Scholarly Publishing Office and the Digital Library Production Service at the University of Michigan, Ann Arbor. The digital reformatting process results in an electronic version of the text that can be both accessed online and used to create new print copies. This book and hundreds of others are available online in the History E-Book Project through subscription.

Many of the works in the History E-Book Project are available in print and can be ordered either directly from their publishers or as part of this series. For information refer to the online Title Record page for each book. Inquiries regarding this series can be directed to info@hebook.org.

ACLS
HISTORY E-BOOK

http://www.history

I0834402

# EPICURUS AND HIS GODS

# EPICURUS
## AND HIS GODS

(*Epicure et ses Dieux*)

*by* A. J. FESTUGIERE, O.P.
Directeur d'études à l'École des Hautes Études

*Translated by* C. W. CHILTON
Lecturer in Classics at Hull University

HARVARD UNIVERSITY PRESS
CAMBRIDGE, MASSACHUSETTS
1956

PRINTED IN GREAT BRITAIN

CONTENTS

## TRANSLATOR'S NOTE

THE original edition of this book was published in Paris in 1946. This translation incorporates many alterations and additions made by the author. Some concern the text but most are to be found in the notes and bibliography and are intended to take account of work published since 1946.

While this version was being prepared the latest addition to the list appeared – *Epicurus and his Philosophy* by N. W. DeWitt (University of Minnesota Press, 1954). Fr. Festugière wishes me to acknowledge his indebtedness to this book for some alterations in the details of Epicurus' early life which have been made in Chapter II.

I am responsible for the index and list of abbreviations.

C. W. CHILTON

MAN is unhappy. From the time of Homer and his reference to 'men of a day' no people has devoted so much thought to this matter as the Greeks. The Greek looked at life without illusion. It was the great theme of human misery which inspired the tragic choruses to their unforgettable laments. The moralists of Greece echoed the words of the poets: 'The whole world', says Epicurus, 'lives in pain; it is for pain that it has the most capacity.'

Pessimism is natural to every man eager for life, once he measures the distance between what he aspires to do and what he actually achieves. But a pessimistic view of things does not necessarily lead to inaction. It may be that the goal is hard to reach, that the conquest of happiness calls for a great effort; but it is precisely this effort which reveals man's glory. He is never so noble, he never asserts so well his quality as a true man as when he shows his strength, whether in withstanding misfortune or triumphing over adversity. A Heraclean strain runs all through Greek thought. The myth of the Dorian hero sprang from the very depths of the race at its first beginnings; ever afterwards, in the feudal Greece of Pindar, in the Athens of Pericles, victorious and overbearing, in the Athens of Conon and Timotheus, defeated by Sparta but still proud and quick to recoup her strength, in the Athens of Demosthenes, then among the philosophers of the Porch and, through them, through the influence which they exercised, in the whole civilized world until the end of Paganism, always, from age to age, Heracles and his labours kept their value as an example. Marcus Aurelius compared the wise man to a rock which the waves cover but do not move (IV, 49, 1); Plotinus reminds the Gnostics that the wise man in this world repels the blows of Fortune by his strength of character (II, 9, 18); Sallustius declares that the richest reward of the virtuous man is the feeling that he has obeyed no one but himself in adapting his life to his principles (*de dis et mundo*, 21).

So the pessimistic attitude to life did not lead in Greece to a doctrine of renunciation; joined to a fine natural courage it rather called forth an ethic of struggle and effort. As long as the city was free this effort displayed itself in the service of the city. When the framework of the city was shattered — a framework which for three centuries at least had given the Greek the means to develop his powers — the break naturally brought about a serious crisis. The conquests of Alexander, followed by the wars of the Diadochi, had overturned the world. The little Greek cities, having lost with their autonomy the right to decide between peace and war, could no longer nourish any thoughts of greatness. In the Athens of the fifth and fourth centuries every citizen was in one sense a prince; Aristophanes might scoff, the dotard Demos did really govern the Athenian Empire. But beginning with Cassander, and especially after Antigonus II, Greece had only one master. If a man wished to play a part in the world he must enter the service of that master, or leave his country and pay court to the monarch of Egypt or Syria. How was he to adapt himself to this new situation? What attitude was he to take up, at least if he meant to live as an honest man and stand by his principles? Must he remain aloof, or act? And if the latter, according to what rules?

That is the problem which the various Hellenistic schools of wisdom had to solve. In the solutions they offered we find some features common to all, and others in which they differed. But they all agreed on one point; in future a man must find the source of freedom in himself. Previously the Greek had been almost exclusively a citizen, and, as a citizen, he had known no master but the law. This law certainly imposed itself on him with absolute authority, but he had made it himself. When a law was proposed, it lay in his power to speak in the Assembly of the People for acceptance or rejection, and even if he did not venture to speak he had the right of voting. And so, under the rule of law, the citizen was free. But now the law was the prerogative of a prince, or of his governor in Athens. Even though in appearance the constitution might retain its outward form, so long as the prince's soldiers occupied the hills of Athens there was no longer any question of real freedom. A man must then find in himself an interior freedom which would liberate him; the life which was *adespotos*, i.e. without a master, is one of the typical expressions of the new wisdom (Epicurus, *Ep.*, III, 133; again Sallustius, 21).

It was not less urgent to make oneself free with regard to Tyche. No doubt the Greeks of the fifth and fourth centuries had felt her blows. Athens, to mention only her, for she was the heart of Greece,[1] had known fearful disasters. But she had always recovered, and the Athenian citizen found consolation for his private troubles in the thought of his country, in the warmth of his love for her and in his eagerness to serve her. Now, there was a city no longer. Men had to face Fortune alone, and at a time when that fickle goddess was dealing her cruellest blows at Greece. 'To laugh at Tyche' (Epicurus, *Ep.*, III, 133) is another maxim of Hellenistic wisdom.

He who wishes to be independent of men and of Fortune must learn to be self-sufficient. The Sage of the third century is a being who is self-sufficient (*autarkes*). This is to say that to be happy he needs nothing but himself. He strives to make himself indifferent, 'insensible' (*apathes*), to everything that comes from outside. He seeks after nothing but constancy of soul, a serenity like the tranquil sea (*galenismos*), like the calm waters of a haven that no current disturbs (*ataraxia*). Such are the features common to Hellenistic sages, to whatever school they belong, Cynicism, Porch, or Garden.

But these schools differed in other characteristics. Let us consider only the two main ones, those of Epicurus and Zeno, and let us see them grappling with the subject of prime importance, the acquisition of happiness. We will begin with the Stoa.

Man wishes to be happy. Now it was a dogma inherited from the intellectual philosophy of the fourth century that every being, to be happy, must live according to its own essence, must obey its own nature. What then is the nature of man? It was again a dogma inherited from the Academy that man is essentially intellect, and that this intellect is of the same nature as the divine Intelligence. That, in the Stoa, must be accepted to the letter; human reason is nothing but a fragment of the divine

Logos. Now since the divine Logos is identical with universal Nature, since, also, to live according to one's nature is to live according to the Logos, to follow one's own nature as a man and to follow the Nature of the Whole is the same thing. Virtue resides in this act of submission. The Sage is then the virtuous man, and the virtuous man is perfectly happy because he lives according to nature. Everything is summed up, then, in an acceptance of Order, or, what comes to the same thing, of Destiny. This alone counts; everything else, health and sickness, wealth and poverty, praise and disdain of men, all is indifferent. The Sage, at one with the stars, contemplates the order of the universe and in that contemplation finds his freedom.

The result of this is that the Sage possesses a rule of action. Firmly convinced that his will is in conformity with the universal will he feels himself fit to govern other men. Nothing could stand in his way because he relied only on virtue and took account of nothing else. So the Stoic morality became the instructor of rulers. If it enjoyed only a slight influence over the Hellenistic kings who for the most part were stark realists, it conquered the Romans; men like Cato and Marcus Aurelius, and any number of provincial governors were moulded by it. In the debate begun at the dawn of Hellenism – 'Must we act?' and 'How must we act?', Stoicism took the side of action and taught a set of rules. That is why it has played so important a part in the history of civilization.

The message of Epicureanism was very different. Man wishes to be happy. Now what impedes his happiness is desire and fear. Desire, because it is infinite and so there is always a gulf between the goal we set ourselves and the one we reach. Fear, because it disturbs our peace of mind. We must then examine our desires and distinguish those which correspond to basic needs from the adventitious kind fostered by social life. In this way we ascertain that the desires which are natural and necessary are very few and need only the simplest things to satisfy them. Next we must banish fear. We live in terror of the gods and of death. Now the gods are not to be feared, because they take no interest in human affairs. And the very instant we say that, the fear of death is expelled. For, at bottom, what we dread in death is not death itself; on this point the Greek was modest, he knew he was mortal and understanding the distance that separated him from the condition of the gods it seemed to him presumptuous to count on an infinite existence. No, what we fear in death is the consequences, the punishments of Hades. But if the gods have no concern with our affairs it is absurd to believe in a judgment after death. Besides, all consciousness disappears when life leaves us. All consciousness and, as a result, all capacity for suffering.

Thus emancipated from empty desires and from fear, man is free. But this freedom does not come without a large measure of self-denial, and one of the first things which the Epicurean must give up is political activity. The reason is obvious. A man only engages in public affairs from a desire for power, wealth, or honours. Now these three desires make him dependent on men and Fortune and disturb his peace of mind. If this peace is the supreme good it is worth any sacrifice; the first condition for obtaining it is to live a hidden life (*lathe biosas*), far from all worry and sheltered from the crowd. This no doubt implies egoism. But we must remember that the city, which previously had stood as the ideal to be followed, had perished, and the individual had nothing to look for now but his own contentment. If this contentment flows from peace of mind we must avoid all the burdens that may spoil *ataraxia*. In the Hellenistic debate between political activity and withdrawal, Epicureanism chose withdrawal. That is where it differs most from the morality of Zeno.

It is noticeable that both doctrines touch on matters of religion. The Stoic lives in accord with the Cosmic god, the Epicurean banishes the fear of the gods and of Hades. Therefore these two systems of morality fundamentally imply a religious attitude. But whereas the attitude of the Stoic is simple and easy to understand, that of the Epicurean is more complex and admits of more subtleties. It seemed to me it would be of interest to examine the problem afresh and to renew acquaintance with the philosophy of the Garden from this angle.

This little book, then, begins with a general survey of Hellenistic religion, at least of one of the principal characteristics of that religion, the decline of traditional beliefs and the birth and growth of the cosmic religion, with its special appeal to the learned.[1] The second chapter recalls what kind of a man Epicurus was. More perhaps than for any other Greek school the personality of the founder is here of the highest degree of importance. Now by a happy chance Epicurus is of all the ancients the one who reveals himself most completely to us, and to our delight we find in him an admirable nature, a combination of strength, gentleness and charm. In the third chapter I have tried to indicate what the living force of his system was and how it happened that it won such fervent disciples and that it seemed to them to be not so much a system as a way of life which brought release and happiness. Finally the last two chapters describe Epicurus' attitude to the religion of his time in the forms which I have mentioned, the religion of the civic gods and that of the God of the Sages.

Thanks to the forbearance of my publisher, whom I take this opportunity to thank, the text is accompanied by lengthy notes and many references. There are two reasons for this. The philosophy of Epicurus has been in recent years the subject of important studies and it seemed desirable to state my attitude towards than. In particular the publication during the last half-century of the Herculanean papyri has much enriched and on some points shed new light on our knowledge of Epicurus, his school and his ideas. These essential documents, however, are dispersed in numerous collections which even the scholarly public has small chance of reading;[2] I therefore thought it would be useful to quote extensively from them. Moreover, these texts are difficult and admit of differing translations; I accordingly felt obliged to reproduce them to the letter. In this way the critical reader will have the means of checking what I have said and, if he wishes, of correcting it.

Paris, Ascension Day, 1945

## NOTES

[1] Ἑλλάδος Ἑλλάς: epitaph of Euripides, *Vit. Eur.*, 135 W.

[2] The substance of these pages has already appeared in the periodical *Vivre et Penser* (war series of the *Revue Biblique*), 3rd series, 1945.

[3] A list of them will be found in the *Bibliography*, *infra* pp. 94.

# EPICURUS AND HIS GODS

CHAPTER I

# THE STATE OF RELIGION AT THE BEGINNING OF THE HELLENISTIC AGE

WHAT is the meaning of the word 'Hellenistic' when it is applied to religion, in Greece and the Greek world? The German historian Droysen in his *History of Alexander* (1833) asserted the existence of an important break in the history of Greece and the world at the time of Alexander: 'The name of Alexander,' he writes, 'represents the end of an epoch and the beginning of a new age.' Of course, Droysen was considering the question from a political angle. Does this break still mean anything from the point of view of religion? It will have a meaning, the word 'Hellenistic' applied to religion will be justified – in short, it will be correct to speak of Hellenistic religion – if we can discern, beginning with Alexander, a certain number of characteristics which set a new stamp on the state of religion in Greece and the Greek world. These characteristics, or at least some of them, I should like to define very briefly. To do so I shall firstly summarize the state of religion in the classical epoch (especially in the fifth century) and then, using that as a background, I shall endeavour to describe the new features in Greek religion which appear with Alexander.

By 'state of religion' I understand the collection of beliefs and rites which express the relationship between man and the divine, this latter expression being used to denote in short those forces stronger than man (τὰ κρείττω) – in Greece personified from the beginning (οἱ κρείττονες) – the action of which the Greek recognized in the world, in social life, and in the life of the individual.

## I. *The State of Religion in the Classical Epoch* (*fifth century*)

(1) In the classical epoch religion has the appearance of being firstly a social matter or more exactly a civic matter. Religion and city are inseparably joined. They are joined in the very

structure of the city. Family, phratry, tribe are essentially defined by common cults, the cults of common ancestors, an eponymous hero, of Zeus and Apollo Patröos. At the examination (δοκιμασία) of magistrates of Athens it was established that the candidate was born of Athenian parents, that he had family tombs in Attica and that he shared in the worship of Zeus Herkeios and Apollo Patröos (Arist. *Ath. Pol.*, 55). Religion and city were so closely linked that there were no professional clergy in Greek cities; the magistrates of the city as such were entrusted with the prayers and sacrifices. It is hardly necessary, on the other hand, to mention the sincerity and intensity of the civic religion at Athens in the fifth century. It is enough to refer to Greek tragedy or to the historians of the time, for example to this moving passage in the *Hellenica* of Xenophon (II, 4, 20–21) where, after the battle of Munychia in 403 between the democrats installed in the Peiraeus and the city dwellers who had collaborated with the Thirty, Cleocritus, the herald of the (Eleusinian) initiates, attempts to reconcile the two sides: 'Citizens', he says to them 'why do you drive us out, why do you want to kill us? We have never done you any wrong, we have taken part with you in the most solemn religious ceremonies and in the fairest sacrifices and festivals. We have danced in the same choruses, gone to the same schools, served in the same ranks; we have endured with you many dangers on land and sea for the sake of the common safety and freedom of both of us. In the name of the gods of our fathers and mothers, of the ties of blood and kinship and friendship — for all these ties unite many among us — out of respect for gods and for men, cease to do wrong to our country.' It is noticeable how in this adjuration Cleocritus calls first upon the ties of religion, for the ties of religion are the strongest of all the bonds of the State. All this is well known and I pass on.

(2) The gods who were thus joined to the city were regarded as protectors of the city. The worship of these gods covered the citizen's whole life, from birth to death.[1] Even so, these heavenly protectors of the city and the citizen were quite unfitted to answer the questions which every thinking man asks himself about the action of the divine in the world, the connection

between the divine and morality, and the meaning of human destiny — all the problems which for simplicity I call *personal religion.*[1]

(*a*) Since the sixth century, philosophers in Ionia and Magna Graecia had concerned themselves with the problem of the origin and arrangement of the Universe as well as that of the changes that occur in it. These first attempts led them to conceive of a material First Principle which by successive evolutions becomes the other elements, or even, in Anaxagoras (fifth century) of a spiritual First Principle, Nous or Mind, which acting on matter (the four elements) produces movement and order in it. Leaving aside the details of the doctrines there grew up a tradition of regarding this substantial and moving First Principle as the divine First Principle, as God. For the thinking mind the problem then arose of reconciling this cosmic Principle with the civic gods who themselves had nothing to do with the organization of the Universe.

(*b*) Going back further still, the poets, Hesiod as early as the eighth century, then Theognis (sixth century) and Pindar (fifth century), had faced the problem of the connection between Zeus and Justice. How does it come about that the unjust man triumphs here below, that the just man is wretched? Is there retribution after death to compensate for present injustices? And that agonizing problem of the Righteous Sufferer of which Attic tragedy is so full! The civic gods gave no answer to these questions.

(*c*) Lastly, other wise men, like Pythagoras (sixth century), or certain religious sects, like the Orphics (the Orphic poems had been collected at Athens by the time of Peisistratus), laid greater stress on the problem of the soul and its destiny, a problem which is unquestionably a personal one and entirely independent of civic religion.

All these enquiries and all these movements met at Athens in the last third of the fifth century, thanks to the teaching of the Sophists. This last third of the fifth century (in Athens) marks the first great crisis in Greek religion, a crisis which already predicted that which was to come in the last third of the fourth century and from which Hellenistic religion was to arise. This first crisis can be defined in its broad outlines as the conflict between civic religion and personal religion. All the fundamentals of the civic religion were called into question under the guise of antitheses or antinomies; law and nature, gods according to the law or gods according to nature (that is to say, according to the personal conscience of the individual who regards himself henceforward as in opposition to the whole), etc. All these antinomies are reduced in the last analysis to this one — individual and city. Many important texts in Plato's *Republic* and *Laws* (Bk. X) show the importance of this crisis in the field of religion. The following are some of the difficulties which confronted the believer. If the traditional gods are inseparably linked to the city, and if the worship of these gods is an institution of Law (νόμος), the gods vary from city to city; they have then only a relative importance and no absolute validity. A second difficulty has to do with the conception of the world. If the order in the world is not due to the pre-arranged scheme of a Mind, but to Chance, if it is by chance that the elements are brought together to form this great frame of the Cosmos, how can we believe any more that there is a Providence which watches over the whole of the Universe? The same denial of Providence is reached by another way; by the consideration of the injustices in this life. Lastly, if, as the poets assert, the gods can be appeased and made favourable by prayers and sacrifices, does it not follow that a man can do wrong without fear at the price of sacrificing to the gods afterwards? In short, according to the argument of the young man in the *Laws*, there are no gods; or, if there are, they take no care of men; and lastly, they let themselves be bribed by presents.

In this conflict between the civic religion on the one hand and the questions which a thinking man asks himself on the other (a conflict for which, for example, the *Heracles* of Euripides is good evidence), it can be said that apparently the civic religion triumphed at first. In 399 Socrates was accused of corrupting the youth in that he introduced new gods and did not believe in the traditional ones; Socrates was condemned and died. His was indisputably a religious trial, a trial for impiety (ἀσέβεια). The charge of impiety recurred on several occasions in the fourth century. It threatened for example Aristotle who, foreseeing the threat, left Athens in 322 for Chalcis in Euboea. In his *Against Ctesiphon*, in 330, Aeschines uses it against Demosthenes. All the misfortunes of the city can be charged to Demosthenes not only because he is a wicked man, a base intriguer, but above all because he is impious and therefore the curse of heaven weighs upon him.[3] If then Athens links her destiny to his she risks being contaminated as by the touch of a sacrilegious and impure being.

But the success of the civic religion was only apparent. In reality personal religion won the day. It won it with Plato who in all strictness must be called the true initiator of Hellenistic religious thought.

I need hardly say that I have no intention of reviewing here the philosophy of Plato. It is enough for me to put the problem and to show that in two characteristics of his system Plato lays down two of the most striking features of later belief.

What the thinking man was looking for was a God who would be at the same time the First Principle of order in things, and the support and symbol of the fundamental concepts on which civilization is founded; Truth, Justice, Beauty, the Good. He wanted, in other words, a God who would be in a full and absolute sense Being, unchangeable Being, true Being. Now it is true to say that the whole of Plato's philosophy is concerned with acknowledging the pre-eminence of this Being, which is the Platonic Idea, and, at the summit of the Ideas, the One-Good which unifies them. This supreme Being is not only the keystone of all rational order; it is, in so far as it is Beauty, the supreme object of love. Lastly, this supreme Being is beyond all perception by the senses and all intellectual comprehension; the only way of communicating with it is by a kind of spiritual contact which transcends understanding. Of this supreme Being there is neither αἴσθησις nor λόγος nor, consequently, an ὄνομα. God is essentially ineffable (ἄρρητος). There is no need to dwell on this nor to show how this definition of the ideal order, this role assigned to love (ἔρως), this transcendant nature of the Divinity was to influence religious thought from the first century of our era beginning with Philo. One of the chief tendencies of religious thought under the Empire, the tendency to work towards a transcendant God by abstracting everything that is material and visible, is derived directly from Plato.

But Platonism did not lead only to the worship of a hypercosmic God, it led also to the worship of a cosmic God, the divine principle of the visible order, of the Cosmos. This is how it happened. The pre-eminence of ideal reality is due to its immutability. The inferiority of visible objects is a result of their incessantly changing. But, among visible objects there are some which always change in the same way, some whose movement is always perfectly constant; these are the heavenly bodies. Now such a movement presupposes a moving Soul endowed with Mind. There is then a divine Mind, mover of the heavens, and this Mind is God. Such, very briefly, is the Platonic doctrine concerning the order of the Cosmos and the cosmic God. Now this doctrine was bound to have considerable influence on Hellenistic religion, precisely from the last third of the fourth century. To make this clearer I must return for a moment to the part played by civic religion in the system of Plato.

Plato had no more intention of suppressing the traditional religion than had Aristotle. In the *Laws*, as in the *Politics* of Aristotle (Bk. VII), when the conditions for the ideal city are being laid down, several paragraphs specify what belongs to the gods; temples, priests, worship, festivals, etc. This is because neither Plato nor Aristotle had yet conceived of any political organization but the Greek city, or of any status for a man but that of free citizen in a State of which the essential governing principle was not the will of a monarch but the law agreed upon by all. But the divorce between this civic religion and personal religion was apparent at once. In so far as he was a citizen, a member of a civic body, a man worshipped the gods of the city. The organization of this worship was left, as in the past, to the oracle at Delphi. Everything was settled in accordance with its responses and with ancestral traditions. But in so far as he was a private person the Sage did not betake himself to those gods; he looked to a transcendant God or a cosmic God, in short, to a God who satisfied the demands of his reason and the needs of his soul. The 'eros' of the Sage led him not to the civic gods but to supreme Beauty or the divine First Mover.

The results of such an attitude can be seen at once. From the very start the divorce between the religion of the Sage and that of the people was obvious. No doubt the Sage did not criticize the worship of the Olympian gods (if there are signs of irony in the *Timaeus* and the *Laws*, as indeed there are, they come rather from a refusal to discuss the matter than from any overt criticism) and, in so far as he was a citizen, he sacrificed according to the rules. But the true religion of the Sage belonged to another sphere. In the second place, it is evident that the principal support of civic religion lay in the city itself. The gods were the protectors of the city in rather the same way as this or that saint in Mediterranean countries (Spain, Italy, Greece) is the accredited protector of this or that town or village. In the *Against Ctesiphon* once more, Aeschines, who is endeavouring to set himself up as a pious man by contrast with the impious Demosthenes, shows himself imbued with traditional piety when he declares (p. 57): 'If the gods will allow it . . . I flatter myself that I shall prove to the court that the city owes its salvation to the gods and to those (Philip and Alexander) who have treated it on certain occasions with humanity and moderation, whereas all its misfortunes have come from Demosthenes.' But this link between gods and city was particularly valuable only as long as the city was autonomous, mistress of its decisions and free to act in accordance with its own views. Then, the city made plans, engaged in enterprises, and it was clear that it needed the help of the gods as much as any ordinary individual who ventured on some private course of action. But should the day come when the city lost its autonomy, no longer constituted a State, but formed part of a bigger State whose monarch would dictate its decisions, than this essential alteration in the status of the city would bring a corresponding change in the civic religion. There might be perhaps no outward sign of change. In A.D. 262–3 under the emperor

Gallienus, the wheeled boat bearing the peplos on its mast was still propelled to the Acropolis, just as it was in the third century before our era[4] and probably had been ever since the sixth. A very great number of the inscriptions concerning matters of religion do not go back beyond the Hellenistic epoch. Besides, it is evident that in all religions nothing is more conservative than worship and the liturgy. But the feeling must have changed. Tradition took the place of the impulse from the heart. Everyone realized that the prayer to Athena was one thing in the mouth of the men who fought at Marathon, another on the lips of the Greeklings.

We are now in a position to consider and understand what repercussions the political events which ushered in the Hellenistic age would have on religion. We have seen two forces opposed, of which one, the civic religion, closely united to the status of the city, was more and more losing its hold over the *élite*, while the other, personal religion, at all events in the form I have indicated, that is, the Platonic religion of a cosmic God, was increasing its influence all the time. The events precipitated by Philip and Alexander would tilt the balance further between these two forces. Let that be said at once to indicate the meaning of what is to follow. There are no doubt, in Hellenistic religion, certain elements which were derived more directly from the political activity of Alexander, elements which that activity, in some sense, partly created. But these are not, I believe, the chief elements. The chief element is the predominance, more and more assured, of personal religion. We must not forget that the religion of the cosmic God soon became part, at the same time as astronomy, of Greek *paideia*, that is, of the intellectual equipment which everyone who aspired to be educated had to have in the Hellenistic kingdoms from the third century onwards. It is enough to recall the remarkable success won by the *Phainomena* of Aratus (second century), a success so great that Cicero in the first century translated the poem for the Latins. Here again, the epic career of Alexander did not create; it hastened a movement which began further back, with Plato. The political activity of Alexander and his successors only removed the obstacles and created the conditions in which the specifically religious heritage of Platonism could more easily expand and develop. Let us see what these conditions were.

## II. *The State of Religion in the Hellenistic Age*

The political consequences of the events which occurred in the terrible last third of the fourth century—let us say from the battle of Chaeronea (338) to that of Ipsus (301, between Antigonus, who was killed in the battle, and his son Demetrius on one side, and Lysimachus and Seleucus on the other)—can be confined essentially to two facts; on one side, the subjection of the Greek cities and its counterpart, the formation of the three great monarchies, of the Lagids in Egypt, the Seleucids in Asia (Asia Minor with a part of Syria and eastern Asia), the Antigonids in Macedonia; on the other, the Hellenization of the eastern world (Egypt and Asia) and the fusion between Greeks and barbarians which Alexander himself began. I shall endeavour to show that these two important facts conspired together to effect the decay of civic religion and the rise of personal religion, especially the religion of the cosmic God.

### 1. *Subjection of the Greek cities to the Hellenistic monarchies*

This subjection, it is true, was not brought about in a day. Under the constitution of the League of Corinth (338) the cities which concluded an offensive and defensive alliance with Philip and his successors kept their liberty and autonomy and, with some exceptions, enjoyed exemption from tribute and garrison. This régime lasted throughout the reign of Alexander (336–323). One Greek city only, Thebes, was in 326 totally destroyed and its population massacred or sold into slavery. Nevertheless, it would be true to say that after 338 the Greek cities were no longer really autonomous. The alliance which they had contracted with the Macedonian princes was a forced alliance; they no longer had the decision in questions of peace and war. The synedrion or, in effect, the *hegemon* of this synedrion, Philip or Alexander, decided the foreign policy of the league, and therefore of the cities which were its members. Besides, Alexander, as his conquests extended, became so conscious of being himself the real master that in 324, without consulting the League, he issued an order from Susa bidding all the federated cities recall their political exiles. In the same year, and from the same place, he instructed the same Greek states to recognize him as a god. Their revolt on the death of Philip in 336 and on that of Alexander in 323 is clear proof that the Greek cities realized full well that they were free no longer. On the last occasion, during the Lamian War, Athens saw her fleet overwhelmed at Amorgos and her army at Crannion (322). From then on she really had lost her autonomy. A Macedonian garrison was installed on the hill of Munychia. More than half the citizens (four-sevenths to be exact; 12,000 out of 21,000) were excluded from citizen rights; many of them were sent as colonists to Thrace, others withdrew into the Attic countryside. Antipater, in 322, established an oligarchic government. Cassander, in 317, took over his father's policy and named Demetrius of Phalerum as high-commissioner in Athens, which remained under the effective control of Macedonian troops (317-307). Conditions would not have been very different if Athens had simply been ruled by the foreigner himself.

Imagine then the repercussions all these events would have upon the individual mind, and especially upon the religious mind. What had become of the divine protectors of Athens, what were they doing, what were they caring for? Here are some significant points.

After Chaeronea, on the epitaph of the Athenian warriors killed in the battle – it can still be read in the Cerameicus – it is not the civic gods who are invoked but impersonal Time which sees all things go by:

> O Time, you who see the passing of all human destinies,
> grief and joy,
> Tell to eternity the fate by which we fell.

When, in 324, Alexander demanded that the federated Greek cities should recognize him as a god, Demosthenes, though hostile to this action at first, ended by advising the Assembly 'to recognize the king as the son of Zeus, or even as Poseidon, if it gives him pleasure'. To quote Wilcken,[5] it is evident that 'in the emancipated circles for which polytheism had lost its meaning, it was no longer possible to become excited over a matter of this kind'. Menander, who lived and produced his plays at Athens in the last third of the fourth century, puts on the stage, in his *Arbitration*, a slave, Onesimus – who in many ways anticipates Figaro – and a testy old man, Smicrines. The latter having mentioned Providence, Onesimus answers him rather like this: 'Think how many cities there are in the world and, in these cities, how many inhabitants. Look at the myriads of persons. Do you imagine that the gods are interested in the affairs of all these people? You want to overwhelm them with cares; that's not a life fit for gods!' Some have tried to find in these words traces of Epicureanism (Epicurus does not deny the existence of gods, he makes of them an order of beings composed of finer matter who live in perfect peace and take no care of human things). I believe myself, more simply, that Menander is here, as in others of his comedies, an accurate witness of that feeling of disenchantment, leaning towards melancholy, which many people of his time felt regarding the gods. Lastly, several years later, there is Euhemerus, who lived for a time at Athens at the end of the fourth century as a member of the circle round Cassander. He also expresses the mood of the times when he shows, in his *Sacred History*, that the gods were originally only men who had been deified as a reward for their exploits and their benefactions. The idea was not entirely new. It derived in part from the tendency, which had always reigned in Greece, to make heroes out of great men. The importance lies in the extraordinary success which this doctrine achieved. It coincided with the first manifestations of the worship of Hellenistic kings, and if, as Jacoby[6] thinks, it was deduced in some measure from that practice, it is probable that in return it encouraged the growth of the practice. The work of Euhemerus was one of the most widely read books of the third and second centuries, and as proof of this let us recall the remarkable fact that from the quantities of Greek works offered to him it was precisely this one that Ennius, in the second century, translated into Latin, thus making the first translation of a Greek book into Latin prose.[7]

It is only right to repeat emphatically that none of this affected the actual ceremonies of worship, or the religion of the people. Far from neglecting the old festivals, the Hellenistic Age, at least in the third century, created new ones; the *Soteria* at Delphi, *Museia* at Thespiae, *Asclepieia* at Cos, *Didymeia* at Miletus, etc., and religious gatherings in honour of Artemis Lycophryene at Magnesia on the Meander, or of Athena at Priene. This was the age which saw the religious ambassadors, the *theoroi*, travelling all over the Greek world to invite the cities to these great acts of worship. What I have said is concerned with inner religious conviction, especially among the educated public; for it is true to say that it is this public which counts in the evolution of religious ideas. It is they who determine the changes; new ideas and new sentiments which begin with the *élite* gain currency afterwards among the masses. I will give just one example. During the third century, Callimachus, whose learned hymns to Zeus, Demeter, Apollo, and Delos are simply literary and antiquarian exercises without any colouring of religion, asserts in a funerary epigram the worthlessness of all the traditional beliefs about the fate of souls after death; there is no Pluto, no Elysian Fields, all that is lies (*Epig.*, xiii). And the inscriptions on tombs show that this scepticism spread wider and wider; in the first century before our era it can be said that beliefs about a life beyond the tomb were regarded by knowledgeable people as no better than old wives tales,[8] and, except in certain religious sects like that of the initiates of Dionysus (who placed an ivy-leaf upon their graves) we must wait until the first or even the second century A.D. to see in funerary epigraphy any signs of the promises of immortality which the oriental religions held out. Note, also, that it was precisely to restore life to polytheism that the Stoics employed allegorical exegesis (this again was not new; Protagoras used it in the fifth century): Zeus is the sky, Hera the air, Demeter the corn, Dionysus the vine, etc.

Then, in addition, there is this all-important fact. The Greek city did not only amount to a political organism; it was in some degree a Church, as a result of the close connection between the political and religious elements. The same word *nomos* (law) signifies at once the civil law, brought into being by a double vote of Council and Assembly, and those traditional customs, those ancestral usages which from time immemorial had governed the behaviour of the citizen in all matters of religion and morality. The city demanded everything from a man. There was no higher aim for him than to devote himself to his city; to devote himself to the city and to devote himself to the city's gods was in reality the same thing. The individual, with his own conscience and spiritual needs, did not go beyond the citizen, he found his complete fulfilment in his duties as a citizen. How was it possible not to realize that, from the day when the Greek city fell from the position of autonomous state to that of a simple municipality in a wider state, it lost its soul? It remained a home, a material background; it was no longer an ideal. It was no longer worth living and dying for. From then on men had no moral and spiritual support. Very many, from the beginning of the third century, left their countries and went to seek work and adventure in the armies of the Diadochi or in the colonies which the latter had founded. Soon, at Alexandria in Egypt, at Antioch in Syria, at Seleucia on the Tigris, at Ephesus, cities grew up which were enormous by the standards of antiquity (2–300,000 inhabitants); the individual was no longer surrounded and supported as he had been in his little native town where all were acquainted from father to son. He became a cypher, like a modern man, for instance in London or Paris. He was alone, and he had his first experience of solitude. How was he going to react? Two features of the Hellenistic age show us very clearly.

The first feature is the diffusion in this age of those religious fraternities which met together for the worship of a foreign god. In the Greek city where he had been born, by virtue of his status as a citizen the man had naturally been a member of a certain number of social groups, family (*genos*), phratry and tribe, where he found established cults which he had simply to follow and which he never thought of questioning because they were the cults of his race. Now, in his own country or outside it, he entered by his own free choice into fraternities entirely independent of the city, the sole link between the members being the worship in common of a foreign deity. I cannot stay now to go into details. What strikes me as essential is the fact that adhesion to Hellenistic religious sects was the result of a free choice by the individual. Nothing compelled him to betake himself to this or that new deity, Isis, the Syrian Aphrodite, the Phrygian Great Mother, etc.; there was no compulsion because these gods were not bound to any city. He was not drawn by custom to worship them. If he went to them, it was from the impulse of a personal religious conviction, to give satisfaction to a need of his soul. That, in religion, is a new and very remarkable thing.

The second feature is the spread of the religion of a cosmic God. Under the influence of Plato (*Timaeus* and *Laws*), of the author, whoever he may be, of the *Epinomis*, and also of the first exoteric writings of Aristotle, the popularity of which was immense, especially of the *Eudemus*, the *Protrepticus* and the περὶ φιλοσοφίας, men took pleasure in recognizing in the beautiful array of the heavens, in the regularity of the movements of the planets (this regularity had been demonstrated by fourth-century astronomers), the manifestation of a divine Intelligence. Besides, since the *Timaeus* it was believed that the human soul by its composition and origin was akin to the soul of the stars; it is from the stars that we come and to them we return after death. Thence the idea grew up of a city of the world, which is the real City, at least for the Sage and the educated man. In the *Protrepticus* Aristotle, following Plato, points to the value and celebrates the delights of the theoretical or contemplative life, that is of the life of study enjoyed by the philosopher or the scholar who meditates on eternal things. Since the earthly city no longer offered any noble aim to live for the Sage took refuge in the celestial city; there he achieved completion in thought and there he found consolation and the strength to bring the movements of his soul into harmony with those of the heavens. This attitude, once again, is the work of the individual conscience.

The disillusioned citizen of Athens, like the Athenian settled in Alexandria, in Antioch, or even in some Macedonian colony in the extreme Orient, could all alike make their escape towards the city of the sky. Let us not forget that we are talking about Mediterranean countries where the night sky shines with an incomparable brilliance.

Now to turn to the second point.

## 2. *The Fusion of Greeks and Barbarians*

We may remember Alexander's memorable act at Opis (a little north of Babylon, on the Tigris) in 324. He had invited Macedonians and Persians to the same banquet. Greek priests and Persian magi had begun the sacred rites. A single cup was passed round the table. Each one drank from it, and poured out a few drops in honour of the Greek and Persian gods. Then Alexander uttered a prayer in which he asked the gods to bring about, between Macedonians and Persians, 'a union of hearts and fellowship in power'. Whether, by this symbolic ceremony, Alexander proclaimed even then a kind of human fraternity between all peoples, as Tarn would have it,[9] or whether he was thinking merely of a fusion between Greeks and Iranians, as Wilcken holds,[10] it is certain that the decisive step had been taken; the old antinomy between Greeks and barbarians, with which Aristotle showed himself to be still completely imbued (*Pol.*, VII), was from thenceforward abolished. The results of this policy, under Alexander himself and his successors, are well known. There were, in Susa in 324, the mass marriages between Macedonians and Persian women; Alexander set the example by marrying, with Persian rites, Statira, the daughter of Darius (he had already, in 327, married with Bactrian rites Roxane, daughter of prince Oxyartes, in the fortress of Choryene in Bactria) while Hephaestion, his most faithful friend, married Drypetis, Statira's sister. There was later, as a product of the Graeco-Macedonian colonies in the East and of the permanent contact between the colonists and the local population which resulted from them, the mixing of the races. The Greeks brought their language, their law, their *gymnasia*, in short everything which their culture comprised and which is expressed by that vast word *paideia*. On their side the peoples of the East placed before the Greeks the spectacle of civilizations a thousand years old, dominated, as a rule, by religion; and in the sphere of religion, the Greek showed himself receptive, ready to worship and accept the divinities of other peoples. This mixing of races and cultures had a great effect upon religion. It helped to widen the notion of the divine. If, as Eratosthenes said a hundred years after Alexander,[11] men must not be divided into Greeks and barbarians, but into good and bad – for, even among the Greeks, there are many bad men, while among the barbarians there are highly civilized peoples like the Indians and Arians and others, such as the Romans and Carthaginians, to be admired for their political qualities – if then all peoples were summoned to merge into one single people, to make one single city, it was because that City in reality already existed: it was the World City, ruled over by the cosmic God. The particular gods of this or that state were only local manifestations of the same unique Divinity who was inherent in the entire universe. Hints of this idea had already appeared at the beginning of the Hellenistic age. We know how it came to fruition. Under Augustus a temple in Rome gave it concrete expression; the Pantheon, whose vault simulates the celestial sphere.

Thus the idea of a universal monarchy, an idea conceived, it seems, by Alexander, revived later by Caesar and realized in the Roman Empire, was itself to lead in the sphere of religion to a lessening of the importance of local particularism and to favour the rise of a universal religion. The first form which this religion took was the cult of a cosmic God. The same Sky was spread over all peoples as over all individuals, however different they might be in race and culture, who lived in the great Hellenistic cities.

So the principal results of Alexander's work – the subjection of the Greek cities, the formation of vast monarchies, and the fusion of Greeks and barbarians – created the conditions which allowed personal religion, more particularly the philosophic religion of the Universe and the cosmic God, to establish itself.

This religion did not take its rise from direct political action by Alexander. Like every really strong religion it took its rise from the needs of the spirit and the soul, from the need for a God who would satisfy at once the demands of scientific thought and the aspirations of the individual conscience. But if Plato was its originator, Alexander did a great deal to ensure its advance. He did a great deal by his work and a great deal also by his personality. One of the creative forces in the religion of Plato is without doubt *eros*, the passionate impulse of love which draws the soul out of its narrow earthly prison so that, going beyond itself, it reaches other shores, another, better, homeland, the world of the Ideas or of the constellations of the Sky. The spiritual movement sprung from Platonism is a flight towards eternity, an escape. Alexander was a stirring symbol of this creative power of *eros*. The urge was always with him to go further, to cross the boundaries which halted him. No sea, no river, no mountain should stand in the way of his prodigious spirit. Many times the historians, such as Arrian, speak of the *pothos*, the irresistible longing for the unknown, the unexplored, and the mysterious, which was bound to take him to the ends of the world. It was this desire which, in 335, drove him to cross the Danube to see what lay beyond it; which, in 331, made him cross the desert to consult the oracle of Zeus Ammon; which, later, urged him to explore himself the lands beyond the Hyphasis, or the shores of the Caspian, or the Arabian coast from the Indian Ocean to the Red Sea. Always to go forward, never to be satisfied with the effort already made, colossal as it was, to reach the confines of the world! This insatiable desire for something 'further' which is always, necessarily, fancied as a 'better', sums up the spirit of the age.

## NOTES

[1] A very interesting book could be written showing the ascendancy of this civic cult over the life of the citizen at Athens, a book on the same lines as c.9 of *l'Histoire du Sentiment Religieux en France* by Henri Bremond (*La Vie religieuse sous l'Ancien Régime*), or the weighty pages of M. Lucien Febure in his recent work, *Le Problème de l'incroyance au XVI^e siècle* (Bk. II, c.1; 'La prise de la religion sur la vie.')

[2] To be more exact, personal religion in its intellectual (or philosophic) aspect; it is this aspect which, as we shall see, prevailed in the Hellenistic age, at least among the educated.

[3] Cf. *In Ctes.*, 77, 101, 106, 125, 131, 150, 152, 221, 224.

[4] Dittenberger, *SIG* (3rd edn.), 894; cf. 374, n. 6.

[5] *Alexander the Great* (French trans., p. 216 = Eng. trans., p. 213).

[6] Pauly-Wissowa, s.v. *Euemeros.*

[7] Cf. also the *Ithyphallus* of Hermocles, for the entry of Demetrius Poliorcetes into Athens in 290: 'The other gods are far away, or they have no ears, or they don't exist, or they take no notice of us even for a second; but you, we see you before us, not in wood or stone but really alive. So it is to you that our prayers are addressed.'

[8] Cic., *Tusc.*, I, 5, 10-6, 12; 21, 48: *N.D.*, II, 2, 5. Juv., II, 149-52.

[9] *Camb. Anc. Hist.*, VI, 437.

[10] *Alexander the Great* (French trans., p. 224 = Eng. trans., p. 221).

[11] Strabo, I, 66, p. 87, 17 (Meineke).

## CHAPTER II

## THE LIFE OF EPICURUS

THE island of Samos, a cleruchy of Athens and the only one which remained faithful to her after the disaster in Sicily, fell at last into Lysander's hands in 404. On its recovery by Timotheus in 363, the Athenians immediately sent cleruchs to it. The first contingent left in 365, another in 362, and a third in 352-1. It was on the last occasion that Epicurus' father Neocles, of the Attic deme of Gargettus, went to settle in the island. Epicurus was born in Samos at the beginning of 341. Besides what he made from his holding Neocles was master of a school; no doubt he undertook the boy's earliest education. At the age of fourteen (327) Epicurus was sent to Teos, which is not far from Samos,[1] to hear the lessons of Nausiphanes. The latter, a disciple of Democritus and perhaps envious of his master's universal knowledge, taught at once philosophy, mathematics and rhetoric. His school enjoyed a high reputation and to it flocked the gilded youth of the coast and the islands, a self-contained, fashionable little community,[2] of which Epicurus does not seem to have retained a good impression. He remained there three years (327-324), until the age of seventeen, and through Nausiphanes made the acquaintance of the Democritean doctrine of atoms and that of pleasure as the ultimate end. Between the 'absence of dread' of Democritus and the 'absence of care' of Epicurus, Nausiphanes' 'absence of fear' provides the middle term.[3]

The cleruchs settled in Samos remained Athenian citizens and, as such, were liable to military service, which lasted two years, in the ephebate. In 323, therefore, at the age of eighteen Epicurus went to Athens where he had as a fellow ephebe (συνέφηβος) the future poet Menander (in 322-1). Aristotle had by then retired to Chalcis, but Xenocrates was head of the Academy. However, his military duties, which included a spell of garrison duty outside the city in one of the fortresses of Attica, can hardly have allowed Epicurus to apply himself to philosophy; this first stay at Athens (323-321) seems then to be of no importance in the intellectual development of Epicurus.[4]

His period of service over, in 321, Epicurus could not return to Samos — for this reason. At the time of the settlement in Samos of the Athenian cleruchies in 365, 362 and 352 the Athenians had expelled the Samian landowners from the island so as to divide their estates among the Athenian colonists. However, in 324, Alexander, by the mouth of his envoy Nicanor had given notice to the Greeks assembled at the Olympic festival that they must recall, in all cities, those who had been banished for political reasons.[5] After Alexander's death (323) Perdiccas, the regent in Asia, carried out this order as far as it concerned the island of Samos (322).[6] The Athenian cleruchs were in their turn driven out and, Neocles having taken refuge in Colophon, it was there that Epicurus rejoined him in 321, at the age of twenty. Thus began his first experience of exile and poverty. Those years so decisive for the formation of mind and character he could no longer spend at the school of a famous philosopher whom he had not the means to pay. He had to live unaided, and unaided arm himself for the struggles of life and the conquest of wisdom. Unlike Plato, Aristotle, and all those fortunate young men who during the fourth century gathered in the Academy, the Lyceum, or about Isocrates, Epicurus was a 'self-made man'. If we remember that he was endowed with a very lively and delicate sensibility, as his letters still prove, if we recall that he was a prey to illness (he had an attack of vomiting twice every day), and that, poor and in ill-health, he had early in life to impose a very frugal way of living upon himself, we have the explanation, to a great extent, both of the strength of his personality — for a man's control over others is the greater when he has been compelled from early youth to get the better of misfortune — and of the peculiar slant of his moral doctrine.

From 321, then, to his settlement in Athens (summer 306), Epicurus lived in Asia Minor, at Colophon to begin with, then at Mytilene in Lesbos and at Lampsacus on the Hellespont. There he worked out his doctrine, which is less a system of thought than a system of life. There also he formed the friendships which were to have so important a place in the school of the Garden. Hermarchus, his first successor, came from Mytilene, Metrodorus and his brother Timocrates, Idomeneus, Leonteus and his wife Themista, Colotes, Polyaenus, and perhaps Ctesippus, came from Lampsacus.[7]

After ten years of solitary reflexion and meditation (321-311), Epicurus, at the age of thirty,[8] began to teach, first at Mytilene, then at Lampsacus where he stayed four years (310-306).[9] Some of the well born and wealthy young friends who had attached themselves to him provided for the financial needs of the school. And so, in complete control of his doctrine, certain of being followed by a group of disciples, and assured at last of his daily bread,[10] Epicurus, in the summer of 306, established himself in Athens. The move need cause no surprise. Without even mentioning other reasons, for example, the fact that Epicurus was an Athenian citizen, this city was then the metropolis of thought. The Academy and the Lyceum had brought it incomparable renown. Anyone wishing to learn how to live in wisdom went there to imbibe his lessons. If a man wished to open a school whose influence should go beyond the bounds of a little provincial city he could consider no other place in which to settle. It was in Athens that the two great beacons of wisdom in the Hellenistic age were kindled, and from Athens that they spread their rays; Zeno, arriving in Athens in 311, founded the school of the Porch in 301, Epicurus purchased the Garden in 306.[11]

From then onwards his life is without history. We know the dates of some of his writings and of some of his letters.[12] We know that he paid two or three visits to his friends in Lampsacus. His health had always been poor. In 270, at the age of sixty-nine, after horrible sufferings caused by an internal complaint and nephralgia, he died in peace of soul. 'This is the happiest day of my life', he wrote to his friends,[13] 'it is the last. The pains in my bladder and stomach, always extreme, continue their course, and lose none of their violence. But against all that I place the joy in my soul when I recall the conversations we have had together. You, who have been faithful to me and to philosophy from boyhood, take good care of the children of Metrodorus.'

This was his last wish. He returns to it in the will which he left. Hermarchus, his successor, and some other disciples must watch over the education of the son and daughter of Metrodorus and of the son of Polyaenus (*Life*, 19-21). He wished them after his death to emulate and continue his care for the poor and the young. He set free his old confidential slave, Mys, as well as three other slaves, one of whom was a woman (*Life*, 20). He asked that care should be taken of Nicanor also, 'just as I did myself', he says, 'so that all those of my companions in the love of wisdom who have provided for my needs from their own resources and who, after showing me every possible mark of love, have chosen to grow old with me in the study of philosophy may lack none of the necessities of life as far as I can prevent it' (*Life*, 20).

Finally, as the annual offerings to the dead (τὰ ἐναγίσματα), like the celebrations of birthdays, were occasions of rejoicing[14] when the common soul of the group opened like a flower, the practice of these rites must be piously maintained, in honour of the parents and three brothers of Epicurus (Neocles, Chairedemus and Aristobulus) and of his friend Polyaenus, as well as on the anniversary of his own birth; there was also the banquet on the 20th of each month to the memory of himself and Metrodorus.[15] Furthermore, so that his friends might give themselves over to joy without hesitation he provided for the necessary expenses in advance by allotting for them a part of the income from the estate he left.[16]

A precious text shows us the spirit in which these banquets were to be held.[17] Those who live a dissolute life (?) must not be admitted,[18] 'nor those who groan in anxiety of soul; on the other hand, those who keep in mind the appearance of the perfect and altogether blessed beings (i.e., the gods) must be invited to feast themselves (εὐωχεῖσθαι) and laugh[19] like the others, not forgetting any of the members of the Epicurean family (τοὺς κατὰ τὴν οἰκίαν) nor indeed any of the outsiders[20] in so far as they are well-disposed to Epicurus and his friends. If we do this we shall not seek to win an empty popularity contrary to the true philosophy of nature (ἀφυσιολόγητον), but, acting in accordance with the veritable laws of nature, we shall call to mind all those who show us goodwill, that they may help us to celebrate the ritual banquets which are right and proper for those who philosophize together so as to attain blessedness'.[21]

'We must laugh and philosophize at the same time,' the master had said.[22] If he intended that after his death his school should continue to enjoy itself on anniversaries, he was not, as Cicero thinks,[23] contradicting himself by attributing to the soul a life after death. The reason is quite different; he wanted to ensure that the atmosphere of joy which he had created among his disciples during his lifetime should not be dissipated when he was gone. And there is no greater joy for men than meeting together among friends to celebrate, in unanimity of heart, the memory of one who was so kind a master.

## NOTES

[1] On the coast of Asia, to the north of Samos. N. W. DeWitt, *Epicurus and his Philosophy*, Un. of Minnesota Press, 1954, puts the stay at Teos after the service in the ephebate (pp. 60ff) and would precede it by a brief stay at Rhodes at the school of the Peripatetic Praxiphanes (pp. 56ff).

[2] μειρακισκεύοντα, p. 414 Us., s.v. Ναυσιφάνης. Cf. Diels-Kranz, 75 A 7, II, p. 247, 15ff with the note; *Epicur.*, fr. 114 Us.

[3] Diels-Kranz, 75 B 2, II, p. 249, 10 τὸ συγγενικὸν τέλος, ὅπερ ἐστὶν ἥδεσθαι καὶ μὴ ἀλγεῖν, *ib.* B 3, II, p. 250, 17 καθάπερ Ναυσιφάνης τὴν ἀκαταπληξίαν (cf. *Life*, 23 ἦν δὲ – sc. Metrodorus – ἀκατάπληκτος πρός τε τὰς ὀχλήσεις καὶ τὸν θάνατον, ὥς 'Επίκουρος ἐν τῷ πρώτῳ Μητροδώρου φησί)· ταύτην γὰρ ἔφη ὕπο Δημοκρίτου 'ἀθαμβίην' λέγεσθαι. So we trace the affinity of the Democritean ἀθαμβίη with the Epicurean ἀταραξία through the ἀκαταπληξία of Nausiphanes. – Epicurus had already at Samos attended the lessons of the Platonist Pamphilus, otherwise unknown. As he left Samos at 14 this teaching can have had little effect on him. Cf. Usener, p. 415, s.v. Πάμφιλος.

[4] Cf. von Arnim, *P. W.*, VI, 133-4. For Epicurus as a hearer of Xenocrates (D.L., 13, Usener, 233), and perhaps of Theophrastus, cf. DeWitt, 50ff.

[5] Cf. *SIG*[3] 306 (Tegea), *OGI* 2 (Mytilene).

[6] Cf. *SIG*[3] 312 (321/0). An honorific decree from Samos for two citizens of Iasos (Caria), Gorgus and Minnion, who were employed, in 322, in returning to their country some Samian refugees in Iasos.

[7] Pythocles also came from Lampsacus, cf. Bignone, *L'Aristotele perduto e la formazione filosofica di Epicuro* (2v., Florence, 1936), II, p. 79, who quotes Philodemus, περὶ παρρησίας fr. 6 Olivieri.

[8] As mentioned above, DeWitt puts the stay in Rhodes and Teos at the beginning of this period, cf. *supra* n. 1.

[9] Cf. DeWitt, pp. 70-7.

[10] The diet was frugal; in 294, during the siege of Athens by Demetrius Poliorcetes, Epicurus and his disciples shared a handful of beans each day. Yet everyone had to be fed. Timocrates accused Epicurus of spending a mina (100 dr.) a day on food (*Life*, 7). This obviously refers to the outlay for the entire community. If we remember that about 300 the value of the drachma had fallen from 6 to 3 obols at Athens and that as a result the price of grain had doubled and gone up from 5 to 10 dr. the medimnus, and other prices in proportion, and if, in addition, we assume that the community of the Garden was numerous, we shall perhaps not be surprised at this figure. On the cost of living in Greece in the Hellenistic age, cf. W. W. Tarn, *The Hellenistic Age* (Cambridge, 1923), pp. 108ff. (*The social question in the third century*), *Hellenistic Civilization*, 2nd edn. (London, 1930), pp. 97ff, and the excellent catalogue in Glotz, *Journ. des Savants*, 1913, pp. 16ff. Note that in 308/7 Epicurus, writing to Polyaenus, asserts that he does not need even an obol for his keep while Metrodorus, who has not attained the same degree of wisdom, spends a whole one on his, cf. fr. 158 Us. (accepting *as* as = obol). It was estimated that a slave cost an absolute minimum of 2 obols a day to keep, cf. Tarn, *The Hellenistic Age*, pp. 120-1.

[11] The date is explained by political reasons. Exiled from Samos by one of Alexander's generals, Perdiccas (cf. *supra*, p. 20), Epicurus was bound to be of an anti-Macedonian tendency (cf. also fr. 101, p. 133, 21 Us.) Besides, he had lived till then in constant rivalry with the school of Plato and Aristotle which enjoyed Macedonian favour. Again, until summer 307, the Peripatetic Demetrius of Phalerum governed Athens on behalf of Cassander. Epicurus, then, waited for the 'liberation' of the city by Demetrius Poliorcetes (10 June 307); he could be sure that in future the rival school would not enjoy so much importance (cf. Bignone, *L'Ar. perd.*, II, pp. 117, n. 1, 130ff). It is possible to be even more specific. After the capture of Athens (June 307), Sophocles of Sunium passed a law forbidding philosophers to conduct a school without the permission of the Council and People (cf. Ferguson, *Hellen. Athens*, p. 104), which brought about the departure of Theophrastus. Such a law would hardly encourage Epicurus to settle in Athens. We must then accept that he did not go there until after the repeal of the law of Sophocles (spring or early summer 306), when freedom of association had again been officially recognized at Athens (Ferguson, pp. 106-7).

[12] Cf. Usener's index, s.v. Ἐπίκουρος, p. 404 and the chronological order of the letters, *ib.*, pp. 132-4.

[13] Hermarchus, Idomeneus, and others. No doubt this short note (fr. 122, 138, 177 Us.) was dictated by the master in his last moments for it to be sent to each of his absent friends.

[14] Cf. Vogliano, p. 44, fr. 5, col. XVIII, 1ff. ἐτάξάμεν ἀξίως Πυθοκλέους τοῦ ἀρίστου καὶ τὰ περὶ τὴν ἐκφορὰν ἐπιλαμπρύναντες καὶ τὰ περὶ τὴν παρασκευὴν τῶν εἰωθότων ἐπι τοῖς τηλικούτοις γίνεσθαι δείπνων.

[15] Cf. Philod., π, εὐσ., p. 104 Gomp. (cf. Diels, *Sitz. Ber. Berl.*, 1916, p. 894) παραγίνεσθαι ἀλ]ηλιμμένον [ἐπὶ δεῖπν]ον, αὑτον τε [ἑορτὴν τ]αύτην ἄγειν (*sic.* Diels: ἀλ]ηλιμμένον ['Επίκουρ]ον αὑτὸν τε[λετὴν τ]αύτην ἄγειν Vogliano, p. 127) [τὴν ταῖς] εἰκάσι. Epicurus seems to have consecrated this feast on the 20th of each month to the memory of Metrodorus and then to his own after his death. But originally it was a feast of Apollo, called Eikadios for that reason (*P.W.*, V, 2098). There was at Athens a college of Εἰκαδεῖς supposed to have been founded by the

hero Eikadeus in honour of Apollo Parnessios (cf. Michel, 974; a decree of the college in 324/3). Diels, *loc. cit.*, p. 894, n. 1 quotes Bacchylides (70, 3: III, p. 216 Edmonds): ὁρμαίνω τι πέμπειν | χρύσεον Μουσᾶν Ἀλεξάνδρῳ πτέρον | καὶ συμποσίοισιν ἄγαλμ' ἐν εἰκάδεσσιν (a skolion for Alexander I of Macedon, son of Amyntas, 498-54). - Here we may note besides that the foundation of a philosophic school at Athens could not be made unless it were established as a religious guild, a *thiasos*, cf. Wilamowitz, *Antigonos von Karystos*, pp. 262ff. (Exc. 2, *Die rechtliche Stellung der Philosophenschulen*). Now a religious κοινόν could not exist without κοινὰ ἱερά, without regular sacrifices, followed of course by a ritual meal (Wil., pp. 274ff). In this way the Academy and Lyceum were *thiasi* of the Muses and we know that in the latter such a ritual meal brought together the 'friends' at each new moon, Wil., p. 84, 15 (Λύκων δὲ ὁ Περιπατητικός) ἐδειπνίζε τοὺς φίλους κτλ. and *ib.*, pp. 264-5. (See also *Stoic. Vet. Fr.*, III, p. 198, 47).

If these ritual meals in honour of the Muses became, in the Epicurean *thiasos* (cf. fr. 414 Us. καὶ τὰ ἱερὰ ἀνακραυγάσματα . . . μετὰ τῶν σεαυτοῦ θιασωτῶν), ritual meals in honour of dead relatives and friends, i.e. funerary banquets (hence the terms ἐναγίσματα *Test.* 18 [cf. K. Meuli, *Griechische Opferbräuche*, ap. *Phyllobolia f. P. V. der Mühll*, Basel, 1946, p. 208], καθαγίζω and συγκαθαγίζω *infra*, n. 21), that in no way alters their religious character. We may perhaps discern, with Bignone, *L'Ar.perd.*, II, pp. 233-42, a parody of these ritual banquets of the Epicurean *thiasos* in the lines of an anonymous comic poet quoted by Plutarch, *c. Ep. beat.*, 16, 1098 C, v. 5-6 ὕμνεῖτο δ' αἰσχρῶς, κλῶνα πρὸς καλὸν δάφνης, ὁ Φοῖβος οὐ προσῳδά but the translation of οὐ προσῳδά ('with an inharmonious song') by Bignone, p. 234 ('non alla guisa dei Prosodii santi') rests on a confusion between προσῳδία (ᾠδή) and προσόδιον (ὁδός), a processional hymn, well known indeed in the worship of Apollo (for example at Delphi, *SIG*³ 450, 4; 698C and at Delos, *ib.*, 662, 8), but having no connection with our text. I also doubt very much whether, in *Life*, 4, the corrupt passage ἅ ἐστι περὶ τοῖς κδ can be read ἅ ἐστι περὶ τοὺς Εἰκαδεῖς (Bignone, p. 240). In spite of what Bignone says, citing Bonitz (*Ind. Arist.* 579 b 20), the accusative after περί would be unprecedented in this sense (especially in the title of a work); besides κδ after the plural τούς would normally be read as 'twenty-four'; lastly τοὺς Εἰκαδεῖς, if it were possible, would mean the religious guild of the Εἰκαδεῖς mentioned above, and not Epicureans who had never borne the name. (Let me say here, once for all, that a number of Bignone's assertions depend like this one on fanciful constructions.) Nor does the emendation τῆς εἰκάδος (Hübner, followed by Usener and Bailey) which assumes a Byzantine abbreviation τῆς κδ seem to me much more likely. It would be better, with Kochalsky, to retain τοῖς κδ as a marginal emendation of Σωτίων ἐν τοῖς δώδεκα τῶν κτλ., an emendation which then passed into the text and irremediably corrupted the following ἅ ἐστι περὶ * * *.

[16] Such foundations are not uncommon in the Hellenistic age. The best known are those of Diomedon of Cos, about 300 (*SIG*³ 1106=B. Laum, *Stiftungen in der griechischen u. römischen Antike*, Leipzig, 1914, II, p. 52, no. 45, a family college in honour of Heracles Diomedonteios); of Posidonius of Halicarnassus, about the end of the 3rd century (*SIG*³ 1044=Laum, II, p. 111, no. 117, a family college in honour of various gods and the Good Genius of Posidonius and his wife Gorgis); and of Epicteta of Thera, about 200 (Michel 1001=Laum, II, p. 43, no. 43, a family *Mouseion* in honour of the Muses and the dead of the family who had been made heroes). Even in the 2nd century of our era a rich woman of Acraephiae in Boeotia founded, not this time by will, a college of 'heroïastai' composed of her son's comrades in the ephebate to honour the memory of this son (and of a daughter)

and to tend piously their burial place (*SIG*$^{3}$ 1243). In general, on these foundations, cf. F. Poland, *Gesch. d. Griech. Vereinwesen* (Leipzig, 1909), pp. 227ff, 272ff, and *passim*, Laum, *op. cit.*, vol. I.

[17] Vogliano, p. 70, fr. 8, col. I, 1ff. On these 'Epicurean banquets', see also fr. 190 Us. and Bignone, *L'Ar. perd.*, II, pp. 170 and 210-11.

[18] The papyrus is mutilated here and the meaning restored by conjecture.

[19] εὐωχ[εῖσ]θαι αὐτοὺς⟨καὶ⟩γελᾶν ὡς κτλ., l. 6. Bignone (cf. n. 3) reads εὐωχεῖσθαι αὐτοὺς γελανῶς, a reading first proposed and then rightly rejected by Vogliano, p. 127.

[20] οἱ ἔξωθεν a term used (with οἱ ἔξω) to denote those who did not belong to the school of the Garden, cf. Jensen, p. 44, n. 3.

[21] ὅπως συ[γκαθ]αγίζωσιν τὰ ⟨τοῖς⟩ἐπι τῇ ἑαυτ[ῶν μα]καρίᾳ συ[μφι]λοσοφο[ῦσι καθ]ήκοντα ll. 19-21; cf. also Bignone, *L'Ar. perd.*, II, p. 210, n. 4, who leaves out ⟨τοῖς⟩, which is not indispensable, and supplies τῇ ἑαυτ[οῦ μα]καρίᾳ. For συγκαθαγίζω in this sense, cf. Damoxenus the comic poet, fr. 2 Kock καθήγισα, speaking of Epicurean banquets.—On εὐωχεῖσθαι, l. 6, cf. (with Vogliano, p. 126), Philod., π. εὐσεβ., p. 104, 8-9 Gomp. καὶ καλέσαν[τα (sc. Epicurus) πάν]τας εὐωχῆσαι. This verb, and the noun εὐωχία are the correct terms for ritual feasts, cf. Plato, *Laws*, II, 666b τετταράκοντα δὲ ἐπιβαίνοντα ἐτῶν, ἐν τοῖς ξυσσιτίοις εὐωχηθέντα, καλεῖν τούς τε ἄλλους θεοὺς καὶ δὴ καὶ Διόνυσόν παρακαλεῖν εἰς τὴν τῶν πρεσβυτῶν τελετὴν ἅμα καὶ παιδιάν, *SIG*$^{3}$ 783 (c. 27 B.C.), l. 34, τοὺς μὲν θεοὺς ἐθρήσκευσεν εὐσεβῶς, τοὺς δ' ἀνθρώπους εὐώχησε πανδήμως, *OGI* 168 (115 B.C.), l. 11 (εὐωχηθεὶς ἐπὶ τοῦ 'Ηραίου), whether speaking of funeral banquets, v.g. *SIG*$^{3}$ 1232 (A.D. 58-59), l. 10 ὥστε τὰς] γενησομ[ένας ἀεὶ]ἐξ αὐτῆς προσόδους εἴς τε ἀνα[σκευή]ν τοῦ μ[νημείου καὶ] εὐωχίαν εἶναι, *CIG* 3028 (=Laum, *Stiftungen*, II, 75, cf. L. Robert, *Rev. Phil.*, 1943, p. 191, n. 10) τούτου κήδονται οἱ ἐν 'Εφέσῳ ἐργάται προπυλεῖται πρὸς τῷ Ποσειδῶνι Ψ . . . ποιήσουσι δὲ τὴν εὐωχίαν μη(νὸς) Ποσ(ειδεῶνος) η' ἀπι(όντος), or of the feasts of colleges, v.g. *OGI* 737 (2nd century B.C.), l. 18-19 ἔτι δὲ καὶ ἐπι τῶν τοῦ πολιτεύματος εὐωχιῶν στεφανοῦσθαι (an order made by Idumean mercenaries stationed at Memphis), or of the feasts of the Mysteries, e.g. at Ephesus, cf. Strabo, XVI, 20, p. 893, 14 Meineke πανήγυρις δ' ἐνταῦθα (at Ephesus) συντελεῖται κατ' ἔτος, ἔθει δέ τινι οἱ νέοι φιλοκαλοῦσι μάλιστα περὶ τὰς ἐνταῦθα εὐωχίας λαμπρυνόμενοι. τότε δὲ καὶ τῶν Κουρήτων ἀρχεῖον συνάγει συμπόσια καί τινας μυστικὰς θυσίας ἐπιτελεῖ, *Brit. Mus. Inscr.* 483, 9 (under Commodus, 180-92) μὴ ἔλαττον ἀναλίσκειν εἰς τὴν εὐωχίαν, 15 ἐπι ταῖς ὁμοίαις εὐωχίαις (*ib.*, l. 10 ἀνάλωμα τοῦ δείπνου. The reference is to Mysteries, cf. l. 2 πάντα περί τε μυστηρίων καὶ θυσιῶν). On εὐωχία, see also the inscription of Antiochus I of Commagene, *Inscr. gr. l. Syrie*, 1, l. 91 with the editorial note. εὐφροσύνη is also found in the same sense, e.g. at Panarama in Caria, cf. *BCH*, LI (1927), p. 73, no. 11, ll. 7-9 καλῶ πρὸς τὸν θεὸν ὑμᾶς καὶ παρακαλῶ καὶ τοὺς ἐν τῇ πόλι τῆς παρ' αὐτῷ μετέχιν εὐφροσύνης (=an invitation to the table of the god), πάντας ἀνθρώπους ὁ θεὸς ἐπι τὴν ἑστίασιν καλεῖ καὶ κοινὴν καὶ ἰσότιμον παρέχι τράπεζαν τοῖς ὁποθενοῦν ἀφικνουμένοις. On these formulae, cf. the commentary of P. Roussel, *ib.*, pp. 131-5. See also Mark the Deacon, *Life of Porphyrius*, 92 ἐποίησεν εὐφροσύνην (meaning a banquet).

[22] γελᾶν ἅμα δεῖν καὶ φιλοσοφεῖν, *Gn. V.*, xli, cf. fr. 394 Us. εἰ δὲ χρὴ γελᾶν ἐν φιλοσοφίᾳ.

[23] Cic., *De fin.*, II, 31, 101.

## CHAPTER III

### EPICUREAN FRIENDSHIP

When Epicurus settled in Athens some of his disciples went with him, others stayed in Asia; but separation did not break the connection. Letters were constantly exchanged. There is a well-known one addressed to 'the philosophers in Mytilene',[1] another to 'the friends in Lampsacus',[2] without mentioning the private letters to one or other of his friends. Three or four times the master paid visits to his communities in Ionia.[3] This warm interchange of friendship is not an entirely new thing. In the Academy also φιλία had been the spiritual bond of the circle and Aristotle, the apostate disciple, could never forget his impressions when, in early youth, he was admitted to the intimacy of Plato. Plato also cared for his absent disciples. He visited them – as Dion and the Platonist group in Syracuse – he wrote to them, advised them, encouraged them to live in real communion with one another. The Sixth Epistle is a good example of his letters of guidance.[4] Hermias, tyrant of Atarneus, and Erastos and Coriscos, settled at Skepsis, are neighbours; let them then form a close bond of friendship secured by mutual ties;[5] in case of disagreement they should refer to Plato himself. What is more, there had been even before Plato's time the circles of Pythagorean friends in Magna Graecia. In general terms it could be said that all the philosophic schools of the ancient world have the appearance of groups of friends.

Nevertheless certain features distinguish the Epicurean 'friends' from their predecessors in Athens or Italy; and these very features reveal the changes which pressure of circumstances had wrought in minds and manners by the end of the fourth century. The Academy contained only men; if a young woman insinuated herself into the circle it was only by a subterfuge.[6] One of the obvious reasons for this exclusion is that the Academy was not so much a preparation for the solitary life of the man of learning as for the active life of politics. It is neglecting the essential core of his work to forget that Plato wanted above all to cure the ills of the body politic. His remedy was that future rulers should also be philosophers, that they should be acquainted with true justice so that they could incorporate it, by means of good laws, in their institutions. Many statesmen went out from the Academy; Phocion of Athens is a typical example.[7] In the Sixth Epistle Plato shows clearly how beneficial would be a union between the statesman Hermias and the two young Platonists who, while undoubtedly well trained in the noble science of the Ideas (τῇ τῶν εἰδῶν σοφίᾳ τῇ καλῇ ταύτῃ, 322d5), still lack experience and knowledge of affairs.

The aim of Epicurus was quite different; so likewise was the purpose of the friendship which he encouraged between his disciples. There is no evidence that Epicurus, a citizen of Athens, was ever interested in the politics of his country. It is true that when a mere youth he had been tempted to take part in them but the misfortunes which afflicted his early years were of a kind to withdraw him finally from affairs. From then on he appears a true man of the new age, a man convinced of the intense unhappiness of life who seeks refuge in *ataraxia*. 'The whole world lives in pain,[8] it is for pain that it has most capacity. It is hardly necessary to prove this for each living thing as the lot of even the higher being does not in any way contradict this universal truth.'[9] If salvation, then, is to be found in the absence of disagreeable sensation it would be absurd to hand oneself over to the disagreeableness of political life. It is this fundamental conviction rather than modesty[10] which impelled Epicurus to keep himself remote from affairs and to live a secret life.[11] This is how he puts it himself: 'Some men have wanted to become famous and highly regarded, thinking that thus they would obtain for themselves security against men. If then their existence is truly secure they have won the good which nature seeks. If it is not truly secure they do not possess that which, following the normal impulses of nature, they longed for at the beginning' (*k.d.*, vii). 'We must free ourselves from the prison of affairs and politics' (*Gn. V.*, lviii).

'It is impossible to live a life of freedom if one acquires great riches because such acquisition is not easy without making oneself a slave of the mob or of kings. But a life of freedom has everything in continual abundance, and if by chance great riches should fall to one's lot it is easy to distribute them and so win the affection of our neighbours'[12] (*Gn. V.*, lxvii). 'Disturbance of the soul cannot be quelled nor true joy created either by the possession of the greatest wealth or by anything else which depends on unlimited causes'[13] (*Gn. V.*, lxxxi).

From this fundamental principle is derived the entire behaviour of the Sage, and in particular his cult of friendship. To begin with, since philosophic education no longer looks to the moulding of politicians, the circle of disciples is open to women, whether married, like Themista, wife of Leonteus of Lampsacus, or courtesans such as Leontion, Mammarion, Hedeia (the Sweet), Erotion, Nikidion, and Demelata. The large number of 'hetairae' may at first sight be surprising and it cannot be doubted that their presence in the school gave rise to some unpleasant rumours,[14] but we must remember that ancient morality was not, in this matter, that of Christianity and that it is only right to judge it by its own standards.[15] To the young Pythocles troubled by violent physical desires a disciple of Epicurus, Metrodorus, writes (*Gn. V.*, li): 'You tell me that the pricks of the flesh lead you to overdo the pleasures of love. If you do not break the laws or offend in any way against accepted good manners, if you do not annoy any of your neighbours, exhaust your strength or waste your substance, give yourself without worry to your inclinations. But it is impossible not to be halted by one at least of these obstacles; the pleasures of love have never profited anyone; it is a great thing if they do no harm' (cf. *Life*, 118).

Besides, these young women would find in the Garden a company where they would be treated as equals, where their dignity as human beings would be conceded. This would be for them an entirely new experience. It is true that the courtesan in Athens at the end of the fourth century was not despised,[16] but even so her condition was far from that of married women. She remained above all an object of pleasure, she was hired, then returned to the *leno*, at will. (Eg. Habrotonon in the Ἐπιτρέποντες of Menander.) The mistress introduced into a man's house without marriage, like Glycera in Menander's Περικειρομένη was liable to be subjected to degrading outrage. Glycera has her hair shorn off by the soldier Polemo in the course of a jealous scene; no Greek would have dared to treat his legally married wife like that. It is easy to imagine then what must have been the feelings of the courtesans[17] in Epicurus' circle, living as they did in a country and an age in which the 'hetaira' was the slave of the married woman. Someone at last allowed them a soul and watched over the good of that soul. It could even happen that Epicurus, struck by the intellectual and moral qualities of a 'hetaira', would entrust to her the temporary presidency which passed in turn to one or other of the disciples. This happened to Leontion,[18] who married Metrodorus.

But the admission of women into the group is only an outward sign. It is not enough to explain the essence of Epicurean friendship. The inner meaning of that friendship is contained in this, that it was not only a means, as in the Academy, but fully an end in itself. In the system of Plato, ἔρως or φιλία is only prized as an intermediary.[19] The feeling aroused by the sight of a loved one should be the starting point of a series of steps forward thanks to which a man is raised to that expanse of beauty which is intelligible Being and, beyond that, to the One which unifies all the intelligibles. The friendship which the members of the Academy conceived for one another will then be felt as a constant provocation to a higher love, the love of wisdom. They will love one another so as to incite one another to contemplation. Love is necessary to dialectic which without it would become eristic. It is necessary to a joint effort where there is a risk of being discouraged. Friendship acquires great value during the progress upwards required from the future ruler; it enlivens, strengthens, and sustains this impulse. But it is not the end. The end is invisible Being and the intellectual contemplation of that Being. Platonic friendship could be compared to the enthusiasm which in a classroom grips the master and his pupils when they are equally in love with good learning – or better still, to the emulation which reigns among novices under the guidance of a pious monk. On the other hand Epicurean friendship is an end in itself. It is not simply an intermediary on the path to wisdom; it is wisdom itself.[20] How does this come about? To understand that we must return to the starting point of the moral doctrine of Epicurus.

Before the evils of life the attitude of Greek wisdom had been previously, and remained for long afterwards, that of patience, a patience inspired not by dejection but by fortitude; the Sage endures the blows of Fortune but he resists and stands firm.[21] But another path can be followed. You can escape from Fortune by adopting a policy of indifference; in this way you avoid giving her the least hold on yourself; it is enough to know exactly the worth of your desires and to satisfy only those which cannot be neglected without ceasing to exist.[22]

In this gradual elimination the first to be met are the desires of the mouth. Nothing is easier than to satisfy them. 'We regard self-sufficiency as a great good not with the intention of living always on little but so that, if we have no large store, we may know how to be content with this little, convinced that abundance is most enjoyed by those who best know how to do without it, and that everything natural is easy to obtain[23] but everything superfluous is difficult. Simple dishes bring us as much pleasure as a rich table if all pain caused by need is removed, and bread and water produce the highest pleasure when a hungry man puts them to his lips.'[24] 'The cry of the flesh is; not to hunger, not to thirst, not to be cold. The man who enjoys that condition and hopes to enjoy it can rival Zeus himself in happiness.'[25]

The Greek, generally speaking, is abstemious, and such percepts have nothing in them to frighten him. But the Greek is intensely interested in honour and renown. The Epicurean sage is equally free from desires of that kind. Not only does he take no part in public affairs,[26] but he does not try to win the plaudits of the crowd in his teaching. 'When I speak of nature I should frankly prefer to play the oracle and cover with obscurity the truths useful to mankind, even though no one were to understand me, rather than conform to common opinions and so gather up the praise with which the mob is so lavish' (*Gn. V.*, xxxix).

'The study of nature[27] does not make men proud, nor producers of empty phrases,[28] it does not bring them to parade that culture which seems so enviable to the crowd; rather it makes them high-spirited[29] and self-sufficient (αὐτάρκεις), and teaches them to take pride in the good things that depend only on themselves, not those that depend on circumstances' (*Gn. V.*, xlv).

'Into old age you have conformed to the model which I exhort you to follow, and you have learnt the difference between studying philosophy for your own sake and studying it for the sake of Hellas. I rejoice with you' (*Gn. V.*, lxxvi).

His own master with regard to his needs, inaccessible to ordinary passions, the Sage, finally, does not let himself be affected by any of the fears which plague the generality of mankind, the fear of the gods, of pain, and of death. This is the best known part of the doctrine and there is no need to dwell on it. It is enough now to recall the 'fourfold remedy' (ἡ τετραφάρμακος); 'The gods are not to be feared, there is no risk to run in death, the good is easy to obtain, the bad easy to endure with courage.'[30] In another climate, with different temperaments, such a system might well have led to a kind of annihilation of the personality similar to the Buddhist Nirvana. If it is true that wisdom consists in extinguishing all desires in oneself, in making oneself indifferent to all incentives to human activity, the ideal would be realized in being totally insensible, totally expressionless and inert. The best life would be that in which one lived the least; it would already be like the sleep of death. However true it may be that such a view of life has its merits, the fact remains that it has never attracted the western spirit and least of all the Greek, and that it has no analogies with the Epicurean doctrine except superficially. The indifference to wealth and honours, the fourfold remedy, all that is only the means to the attainment of *ataraxia*. *Ataraxia* does not comprise in itself all happiness. It is the indispensable condition; it is impossible to be happy if you are in pain of body or mind. But there is a positive content to bliss; negative terms which mark the absence of worry, fear, or pain (ἀταραξία, ἀφοβία, ἀπονία) are counterbalanced by positive terms which denote a state of physical or spiritual joy (ἐυθυμία[31], χαρά, εὐφροσύνη[32]). Those active pleasures will obviously not be such as depend on men or circumstances – without which we should relapse into uneasiness of soul since those pleasures, depending on others, might fail and we should suffer from their failure. They will be such as the Sage can always obtain for himself and such as conform to the idea of 'self sufficiency'. They will be, then, above everything spiritual pleasures.

But what is the nature of these pleasures? To ask that is to raise the problem of the 'way of life' which most befits the Sage and we know that Epicurus had written a book on this subject (Περὶ βίων). Some years before Epicurus, Aristotle, in the *Protrepticus*, had shown how far the life of study and contemplation is superior to the life of the politician or the man of affairs. It must seem at first glance that the philosopher of the Garden shares that opinion. 'Epicurus', we are told, 'was the most prolific of writers and surpassed all authors in the number of his works. There exist more than three hundred volumes by him, and all of them are the expression of his own thoughts without any borrowing from others.' Only Chrysippus looked like equalling Epicurus in this respect – Carneades called him a ravening worm nourished on the books of his rival – but his writings were full of quotations, like those from Zeno and Aristotle (*Life*, 26-27). The author of the Περὶ φύσεως in thirty-seven books and of many other writings on similar themes cannot really have regarded 'the study of nature'[33] as an entirely pointless occupation. Did he not himself tell Menoeceus that one should never cease to study philosophy? 'A young man should not put off the study of philosophy, nor when old should he grow weary of it. For it is never too early or too late for a man to concern himself with the health of his soul. To say that the time to devote oneself to philosophy has not yet come or has passed is to say that the time to be happy has not yet come or has gone. And so there is a duty to study philosophy both for the young man and the old.'[34] To meditate[35] without ceasing on the things which bring happiness, to meditate on them day and night, by himself or with a companion like himself, that, thought Epicurus, is the essential obligation for the Sage.

But we must define exactly what is meant by this life of study and what it comprises. In the first place it not only does not include but positively excludes everything which the Greeks understood by the word παιδεία, that is, all the liberal arts; this at once marks out a radical difference between Epicurean Wisdom and that, for instance, of Plato and Aristotle. 'Launch your boat, blest youth,' the master writes to the young Pythocles, 'and flee at full speed from every form of culture' (fr. 163 Us.). The Epicureans were regarded in antiquity as enemies of learning — 'Those who have shown the most thorough-going opposition to learning are, it would seem, the Epicureans, either because they really believe that learning contributes nothing to the perfection of wisdom, or, as some suggest, because they hope in this way to cover up their own ignorance (in fact the ignorance of Epicurus in many matters is flagrant) or perhaps because the difficult studies of the disciples of Plato, of Aristotle, and of others like them, get on their nerves' (fr. 227 Us.). Cicero also tells us that this exclusion extended to all the liberal arts;[36] 'Does Epicurus strike you as something less than learned? That is because in his judgment no learning counts which does not contribute to the art of living happily. Shall the Sage waste his time in reading the poets who offer no solid food and bring nothing but a childish enjoyment? Shall he be like Plato and spend himself in the study of music, geometry, arithmetic, and astronomy — studies which, starting from false principles, cannot be true sciences and which, even if they were true, would not help us at all to live more happily, that is, to live better? While cultivating those arts must he abandon that other art which is so important, so exacting, and yet so fruitful — the art of living? Let us then not call Epicurus ignorant but those people foolish who think they should pursue till old age studies which it would have been disgraceful for them not to have undergone in their early years.'

In the second place, if there remains for the Sage a certain number of indispensable studies, these still do not by themselves amount to wisdom. They only prepare for it by removing the obstacles which prevent the attainment of happiness. This is true of the 'Physics' and of the 'Canonic' which depends on the 'Physics'. The texts are quite explicit on this point: 'If we were in no way tormented by our suspicions about the phenomena in the heavens,[37] or on the subject of death, fearing lest in some way it concerns us,[38] and further by our inability to grasp the limits of sufferings and desires, we should have no need of the study of nature (φυσιολογία)' (*k.d.*, xi). 'A man cannot free himself from fear about the most essential matters if he does not know exactly the nature of the Universe, but attributes some slight element of truth to mythological tales. It is therefore impossible to obtain our pleasures in a pure state without the study of nature' (*k.d.*, xii).

'It is no use making ourselves secure in relation to men if things above and those beneath the earth, and in general anything in the boundless universe, remain for us matters of suspicion' (*k.d.*, xiii).[39]

'Firstly we must understand clearly that the knowledge of celestial phenomena, considered either in connexion with other doctrines or by itself, has no other object but peace of mind and a sure confidence, as that is the aim of all other studies' (*Ep.*, II, 85; cf. *Ep.*, I, 78-82).

We can now define to what extent the study of nature is called a part of blessedness: 'Moreover we must consider that the proper function of the study of nature is to determine exactly the cause of the most essential matters (τῶν κυριωτάτων), and that our happiness in the knowledge of celestial phenomena lies in just this, and in our understanding of the nature of the bodies observed in these phenomena and of all other facts susceptible of the same exact knowledge which is required by our happiness.'[40]

To sum up, happiness lies in peace of mind. The primary conditions for peace of mind are the limitation of desires – hence the detachment from wealth and honours – and a firm confidence as regards the gods, pain, and death. This confidence cannot be won except by an exact knowledge of nature. The study of nature which removes the reasons for fear has then no value except as a propaedeutic. As such, however, it is indispensable to the attainment of happiness.

But, it will be asked, if the study of nature does not constitute the essence of happiness, of what does happiness specifically consist? Without doubt the absence of pain and worry constitutes in itself pleasure because there is no such thing, in Epicurus' view, as a neutral state.[41] However, we cannot without playing upon words maintain that this negative state (ἀ-πονία, ἀ-ταραξία) supplies any positive content to the idea of blessedness. Besides, the very teaching and example of Epicurus compel us to look for something more. The letter to Menoeceus exhorts young and old to meditate always. In physical suffering the Sage consoles himself with the memory of joys gone by (fr. 121-122 Us.). And he goes so far as to say, in one of his aphorisms (*Gn. V.*, xxvii): 'In other occupations the fruit is gathered painfully when all the work is done: but in the practice of wisdom (ἐπι δὲ φιλοσοφίας) pleasure (τὸ τερπνόν) goes hand in hand with knowledge. We do not enjoy after we have understood but understanding and pleasure come at the same time.' The discussion then turns on the sense we give to this 'practice of wisdom'. In the rival schools, in particular those of Plato and Aristotle, philosophy implied a long course of studies from rhetoric to the science of numbers, shapes, and the heavenly bodies. As we have seen, Epicurus never ceased to proclaim the futility of such studies. They are of no use towards living well.[42] Besides, to follow them is to court the praise of the common man; it is a grand thing to pass as an expert. 'Let others', he retorts, 'of their own free will follow us with their praise; our only concern must be with the healing of our souls' (ἡμᾶς δὲ γενέσθαι περὶ τὴν ἡμῶν ἰατρείαν, *Gn. V.*, lxiv).[43]

That is the important point. Wisdom means a life of the spirit and the exercise of wisdom is the practice of that life. But Epicurus was too much a Greek to think that the healing of the soul could be achieved in solitude. A man needs a physician, he must feel the warmth of friendship about him; thus there must be established that ideal partnership of a master with his disciples. Besides, Epicurus was well aware that he was this Master and ever since the time when he was in Mytilene and Lampsacus he had seen young disciples flock to him in ardent devotion. That is why, in his view, friendship forms an integral part of wisdom. The exchange of thoughts and the support derived from mutual affection no longer serve only to give mutual strength during the pursuit of abstract learning, they are the end in themselves; in these heart to heart exchanges lies that peace of the soul which is perfect happiness. Both the sayings of the Sage about friendship and his conduct towards his disciples show how important is the part played by Epicurean friendship.

Let us begin by considering the texts.

(1) 'The well-born man occupies himself chiefly with wisdom and friendship; of these the one is a mortal good, the other an immortal good' (*Gn. V.*, lxxviii).[44]

(2) 'Of all the things which wisdom provides to make life entirely happy, much the greatest is the possession of friendship' (*k.d.*, xxvii).

(3) 'Friendship joyously leads her dance round the world. Like a herald she trumpets forth the cry to us all: "Awake and congratulate one another" ' (*Gn. V.*, lii).[45]

(4) 'Friendship must always be sought for itself though it has its origins in the need for help' (*Gn. V.*, xxiii). Cf. *Life* 120: 'The necessities of life give rise to friendship; it is indeed necessary to lay its foundations[46] (in fact we sow the ground [in order to reap the crop]). But friendship is formed and maintained by community of life among those who have obtained fulness of pleasure.'[47]

(5) 'That which helps us in friendship is not so much the help our friends give as our confidence in that help' (*Gn. V.*, xxxiv).

(6) 'Neither is the man who is always looking after his own interests a friend, nor he who never associates interest with friendship; for the one trades in favours so as to profit from them, the other cuts off at the root all good hope for the future'[48] (*Gn. V.*, xxxix).

(7) 'The same conviction which has made us confident that

no evil lasts for ever or even for a long time perceives also that the unshakable solidity of friendship rests particularly on this limitation of the evils in life'[49] (*k.d.*, xxviii).

(8) 'Too much haste and too much slowness in forming a friendship are equally blameworthy: we must be ready even to run risks to preserve friendship' (*Gn. V.*, xxviii; cf. fr. 546 Us.).[50]

(9) 'The Sage suffers no more when he is tortured himself than when he sees his friend put to the torture' (*Gn. V.*, lvi).

(10) 'Let us mourn our friends not with lamentations but by keeping their memory in our hearts' (*Gn. V.*, lxvi).[51]

(11) 'That also is very beautiful, the sight of those near and dear to us, when to the ties of blood is joined a union of hearts; for such a sight is a great help to intimacy' (*Gn. V.*, lxi).[52]

Of these texts,[53] nos. 1-3 underline the excellence of friendship, nos. 4-6 define its nature, and nos. 7-10 show how strong true friendship is and to what lengths it should go. But, taking it as a whole, what is the meaning of Epicurean friendship? Here again we must observe that it is a sign of the times; an understanding of the needs of the times will help us to divine its true nature.

The end of the fourth century was a time of great moral confusion. On the one hand, the city having lost the free enjoyment of its independence, the framework of the State, of which it was possible to say that it had the rigidity of a Church, was weakened and less able to support the individual, to guide him or to fortify him in case of need. Besides, the bonds of the family were no longer as strong in Greece as they had been. On the other hand, the framework of State and family were weakened at a time when the analysis of all the subtleties of thought and feeling,[54] already carried to extremes, had led to an over-refined state of civilization which could only make consciences more sensitive and, therefore, more uneasy. Man was supported no longer, he felt himself to be alone; and in this condition he became a prey to scruples, remorse, and spiritual disturbances which he felt more keenly than before.[55] It would not be long before there would be a need for moral direction, before the Sage would be essentially a spiritual director.[56] Epicurus had been ideally prepared for the task. No one had endured more of the political upheavals of the times. At the age of nineteen he was driven from his home and compelled to earn his bread laboriously in exile. He had been obliged, without a teacher, to build up for himself a body of wisdom. All men aspired to happiness, yet this universal aspiration was constantly thwarted. Why was this so? Was it not because, until then, men had entertained a false notion of happiness? Epicurus solved the problem for himself by the doctrine of *ataraxia*; he found salvation, and as a consequence he wanted to make himself the saviour of mankind,[57] and in particular of the young.

The young, in fact, flocked to him. Adolescence is the age of great spiritual crises and we have plenty of proof that young Greeks were in this respect like their fellows in all times. But it is curious to note how the evidence increases at the beginning of the Hellenistic era.[58] Polemo, going drunk into a room where Xenocrates is talking about temperance, is charmed[59] by this teaching and gives himself body and soul to philosophy.[60] Metrocles wishing to be left to die following a lapse of taste,[61] shuts himself up in a house; there he is visited by Crates[62] who consoles him and finally wins him over to wisdom. Then there is the young man whose conversion was thus described by a comic poet, perhaps Menander:

'I'm alone here; there'll be no one to hear what I'm going to say. Believe me, my friends, all the time that I've lived up to now has been death rather than life. I never used to make the least distinction between what is beautiful, good and holy, and what is evil; so thick was the darkness which for so long weighed on my understanding, hiding from me all these truths and veiling them from my eyes! But now that I've come here (to Athens) I've come back to life for the rest of my days, just as if I'd slept in the temple of Asclepius and he'd saved me. I walk, I talk, I've recovered the use of my reason. This sun, so big and beautiful, I've discovered now, my friends, for the first time; for the first time today I am seeing you in a pure light, you, and this sky, this acropolis, this theatre.'[63]

Such is the spiritual atmosphere, if I may use the expression, into which we must replace Epicurus if we are to understand the real meaning of his influence. He also was before everything a doctor of the spirit. In fact, as Usener has shown,[64] several of the Principal Doctrines and a very large number of the maxims scattered in the fragments have been extracted from letters of direction and we should really take account here of the whole corpus of Epicurean Wisdom. Nevertheless, some examples are more characteristic than others.

On a previous page we have seen Epicurus reassuring and, at the same time, warning a young man tormented by desires of the flesh.[65] In another letter to which Philodemus refers, he addresses warm reproaches, we do not know why, to young Apollonides.[66] He even urges a little boy 'to be good':[67]

'We have reached Lampsacus safe and sound, Pythocles, Hermarchus, Ctesippus and I, and we have found Themista[68] and the other friends in good health. I hope that you also are well, you and your mamma, and that you are always obedient to papa and Matro, as you used to be. Be sure, (.)apia, we love you dearly, the others and I, because you are obedient to them in everything.'

Σε μέγα φιλοῦμεν. This affection of Epicurus for his young disciples appears again in other letters. To Pythocles, radiant with youth and beauty (ὡραῖον ὄντα, *Life*, 5),[69] he writes: 'I want to settle myself comfortably to wait for your dear and divine presence' (fr. 165 Us.). Elsewhere (fr. 161a, p. 346, 16 Us.) he compares him to the Good Fortune whose unexpected visits are a delightful blessing. He entrusts this youth to the protection of Polyaenus and takes care that Idomeneus does not give him too much money: 'If you want to make Pythocles rich do not add to his means but take away some of his desires.'[70] He takes care also, as we have seen, that on his death the son and daughter of Metrodorus, and the son of Polyaenus, shall be looked after (*Life*, 19-20). Should it surprise us that the young responded to his affection? The most typical case is without doubt that of Colotes. He was one of the disciples who from the very beginning, at Lampsacus, had gathered round the Master. A close friendship bound him to Epicurus, who addressed him freely with the diminutives Κωλωτάρας and Κωλωτάριον.[71] Then one day when Epicurus was speaking about nature (φυσιολογοῦντος) Colotes suddenly fell at his knees, 'In your reverence for what I was saying at the time you were seized by a desire, not at all in keeping with our philosophy of nature (ἀφυσιολόγητον),[72] to embrace me and clasp my knees, and to give me all that kissing[73] which certain people use in their devotions and prayers. So I was compelled to pay you the same sacred honours and the same marks of reverence . . . Go on your way then as an immortal god and think of us too as immortal' (fr. 141 Us.). Like Apollodorus in the circle of Socrates,[74] Colotes was one of those natures which feel the need to give active expression to their emotions. For him Epicurus is a god and he greets him as a god: 'Do but appear, Titan, and all else is darkness.'[75] The Master smiled – a hint of reproof is clear in ἀφυσιολόγητον and irony shows through in the end of the letter – but he did not fail to understand this youthful fervour. He knew that one of the most deeply felt needs of adolescence is to find a guide whose word and example shall be law, and that there is no greater joy at that age than enthusiasm for a master; 'The veneration for a Sage is a great blessing for those who venerate him' (*Gn. V.*, xxxii). Did he not himself liken the Sage to a god among men?[76] Besides, the life he lived, the completely confident authority of his doctrine, and his unshakable firmness in face of all the blows of fortune gave the impression that he was more than a man; 'The life of Epicurus, when compared with that of other men for graciousness of manner and independence of external needs, could be taken for a legend' (*Gn. V.*, xxxvi). That was how they spoke among the first generation of disciples.[77] Long afterwards, Lucretius re-echoes this praise (V, 8ff); 'He was a god! Yes, Memmius, only a god could have been the first to discover that way of life which today we call Wisdom.'[78]

We are now in a better position to understand the meaning of the friendship which in the School bound the Master to his disciples and the disciples to each other. Sheltered from the world and the buffetings of Fortune,[79] this little group had the feeling that they had reached harbour. They nestled down together under the protection of the Sage whose words were received as oracles. There was no more need to doubt or to re-examine their problems; Epicurus had resolved them once for all. It was enough to believe, to obey, and to love one another; 'O way open, and easy, and quite straight.'[80] Since they had no care left but to strive to understand better what the Master had said, friendship was not only, as it had been in other schools, a stimulus in the course of research; it became the primary pursuit of the elect. Each one had to work to build up the atmosphere in which hearts would open like flowers. It was a question before everything of being happy, and the mutual affection and the confidence with which the disciples relied upon each other contributed more than anything to that happiness. Undoubtedly the Epicurean circle could not escape the faults common to cliques. They regarded themselves as superior to other men and a spirit of adulation reigned.[81] But it appears that Epicurean friendship remained the chief attraction of the School until well on into the Empire. Diogenes of Oenoanda and Lucian,[82] in the second century, bear witness to the strength of the sect. As the latter can scarcely have availed itself of the Master's Physics, we must conjecture that its merits lay elsewhere. Epicureanism was a spirit much more than a doctrine, a spirit embodied in the closely-knit circles whose members scrupulously preserved the words of the Master and made a cult of friendship. In a world where the frameworks of city and family were tending to disappear, Epicurus had succeeded in founding a new family. We may be sure that there lies the secret of his long-lasting fascination.

## NOTES

[1] Fr. 111-14 Usener. On this letter see the important study of Bignone *L'Arist perd.* II, pp. 42ff, 112ff. It was, he says, written from Lampsacus, *ib.*, pp. 78, 113-14.

[2] Fr. 107-10 Us.

[3] δὶς ἢ τρὶς εἰς τοὺς περὶ τὴν 'Ιωνίαν τόπους πρὸς τοὺς φίλους διαδραμόντα, *Life*, 10. Cf. the letter to a little boy fr. 176 Us. = Vogliano, p. 49 (V. however ascribes the letter not to Epicurus but to Polyaenus, *loc. cit.*, pp. 116-18), cf. *supra*, p. 40. It is impossible not to compare the interest which Epicurus felt in his communities in

Asia with the care taken by the apostle Paul of his 'churches'. On both sides similar occasions gave rise to an interchange of letters. Points of doctrine had to be settled – hence the great fundamental letters to Herodotus and Menoeceus (the letter to Pythocles would seem to have been put together from the π. φύσεως: only the beginning is genuine, cf. Usener, pp. xxxvii-ix). Or perhaps the communities are in trouble; the apostate Timocrates who has insinuated himself into the circle at Lampsacus is spreading scandalous libels against the master and his disciples (cf. Jensen, *op. cit.*). Or again, there are short letters of guidance and friendship.

[4] On the authenticity of Epistle VI cf. Jaeger, *Aristoteles*, pp. 112ff.

[5] πειρᾶσθαι ταῖς ἀνθέξεσιν ἀλλήλων εἰς μίαν ἀφικέσθαι φιλίας συμπλοκήν, 323b 1-2.

[6] The Arcadian Axiothea, after reading a part of the *Republic*. Cf. Arist. *Nerinthos*, fr. 64 Rose.

[7] Bernays, *Phokion u. seine neueren Beurteiler* (Berlin, 1881), pp. 44ff, throws much light on what Phocion owed to his development in the Academy.

[8] On the meaning of πόνος in Epicurus, cf. Jensen, *loc. cit.*, p. 35, n. 4.

[9] Jensen, fr. 1.

[10] ὑπερβολῇ γὰρ ἐπιεικείας οὐδὲ πολιτείας ἥψατο, *Life*, 10.

[11] λάθε βιώσας, fr. 551 Us.

[12] And so make friends of them, which is the highest good. Cf. Bailey, *ad loc.*

[13] οὔτ' ἄλλο τι τῶν παρὰ τὰς ἀδιορίστους αἰτίας. Unlimited causes can only be psychological causes, in this case the boundless desire which prevents us from ever being satisfied, cf. Us., fr. 548 and ff. For the meaning of παρά cf. *L.S.J.*, s.v., III, 7.

[14] Cf. Usener, p. 402, s.v. Δημηλάτα.

[15] Extract from a letter of Metrodorus to Pythocles, cf. Pap. Herc. 16369, edited by Vogliano, *Stud. it. di filol. class.*, 1936, pp. 267ff. Μητρόδωρος Πυθοκλεῖ χαίρειν. Πυνθάνομαι κτλ. See also C. Diano, *Epicuri Ethica* (Firenze, 1946), p. 140, 7ff.

[16] As she was to be at Rome, where the very word 'scortum' (literally a hide) used to denote a courtesan is infinitely more brutal than ἑταίρα (companion).

[17] The names (which are in fact pet-names) of many of these young women indicate a servile origin.

[18] Cf. Jensen, p. 12, col. II, 12ff. (The god Asclepius is speaking to Epicurus.) 'Now as to the insults which he (Timocrates) has brought together against you, he does not even succeed in slandering you when he calls it disgraceful for you all that Leontion should have received for a short time (διὰ χρόνου: Jensen renders, wrongly I think, "nach einer weile" and comments, p. 47, "nicht lange nach ihrem Eintritt") the presidency over the other disciples, nay, even over a married woman (Themista). He has no right to laugh at such things and in trying to bring dishonour on you he is dishonoured himself. The presidency can be given to anyone since they alone exercise in turn the function of arbitrator (διαιτήσωσι) and there is no danger of their being treated with contempt by an arbitrator who does not share their tastes.'

[19] Love as an 'intermediary': cf. Plato, *Sympos.* 201e 7-202b 4. For love as a 'collaborator' in the attainment of the Vision of the Beautiful (which is the supreme end): *ib.* 212b 3 τούτου τοῦ κτήματος (the attainment of the θεωρία of the Beautiful) τῇ ἀνθρωπείᾳ φύσει συνεργὸν ἀμείνω Ἔρωτος οὐκ ἄν τις ῥαδίως λάβοι.

[20] Usener, *Kl. Schrift.* I, pp. 305-9, has skilfully analysed the psychological causes of Epicurean friendship. See also Bignone, *L'Ar perd.*, II, pp. 287-303.

[21] Cf. *L'enfant d'Agrigente*, pp. 9ff: *La Sainteté*, chap. II, pp. 27-68, and my article 'Ὑπομονή *in the Greek Tradition*, ap. *Rech. Sc. Relig.*, XXI (1931), pp. 477-86.

[22] Desires natural and necessary; desires natural and not necessary; desires which are only the product of a frivolous fancy, *k.d.*, xxix. Cf. *k.d.*, xxvi, xxx, *Ep.* III, 127.

[23] Cf. *k.d.*, xv, xxi, *Gn. V.*, xxv.

[24] *Ep.* III, 130-1. Cf. *Gn. V.*, lxviii, fr. 473 and ff. Us.

[25] *Gn. V.*, xxxiii. Cf. *Ep.* III, 135 to end and fr. 602 Us.

[26] Cf. above and *Life*, 119 οὐδὲ πολιτεύσεται (ὁ σοφός) ὡς ἐν τῇ πρώτῃ Περὶ βίων. On this scorn of honours and reputation, cf. *k.d.* vii (ἔνδοξοι καὶ περίβλεπτοι κτλ.), *Gn. V.*, lxxxi (ἡ παρὰ τοῖς πολλοῖς τιμὴ καὶ περίβλεψις) and Bignone, *L'Arist. perd.* II, pp. 255-6.

[27] In the sense understood by Epicurus.

[28] οὐ κομποὺς (sic Vat. and Bignone, *L'Arist. perd.*, II, p. 172, n. 1: κόμπου edd.) οὐδὲ φωνῆς ἐργαστικοὺς . . . φυσιολογία παρασκευάζει. Cf. (with Th. Gomperz, *Wiener Studien*, X (1888), p. 206), Eurip., fr. 512 φωνὴ καὶ σκιὰ γέρων ἀνήρ.

[29] Retain σοβαροὺς with Bignone, *Epicuro*, p. 156, n. 3, *L'Arist. perd.*, I, p. 109, n. 1, II, p. 172.

[30] καὶ πανταχῇ παρεπόμενον ἡ τετραφάρμακος· ἄφοβον ὁ θεός, ἀνύποπτον ὁ θάνατος, καὶ τἀγαθὸν μὲν εὔκτητον, τὸ δὲ δεινὸν εὐεκκαρτέρητον (for εὐεγκαρτέρητον), Philod. πρὸς τοὺς σοφιστάς (Pap. Herc. 1005, col. IV, l. 10, p. 87 Sbordone (Naples, 1947)), cf. Crönert, *Rh. Mus.*, LVI, p. 617, *Kolotes*, p. 190. For εὐεκκαρτέρητος, see also Philod., *De Dis*, I, col. 12, 26 (p. 21 D.), 13, 9 (p. 22 D.): τά[ηδ]ὲς εὐεκκαρτέρητόν ἐστι καὶ τἀγαθὸν ὅσ[ον ἐκ τῶν ὑπqκειμ]ένων ε[ὐεκ]πλήρωτον. The opposite is δυσεκκαρτέρητον or ἀνεκκαρτέρητον (κακόν), *De Dis*, I, col. 12, 6 (p. 20 D.)—For the idea, see again *Ep.* III, 133ff, *k.d.*, i-iv, *Gn. V.*, i-iv.

[31] εὐθυμία, a specifically Democritean word (cf. Diels-Kranz, *Index*, s.v.) is not found in the works of Epicurus but in a maxim of his preserved in the inscription of Diogenes of Oenoanda, fr. lvi W. (fr. 9 Usener, who referred this maxim to the letter from Epicurus to his mother (fr. lxiii-lxiv W.)) οὐδὲν οὕτως εὐθυμίας ποιητικόν, ὡς τὸ μὴ πολλὰ πράσσειν μηδὲ δυσκόλοις ἐπιχειρεῖν πράγμασιν μηδὲ παρὰ δύναμίν τι βιάζεσθαι τὴν ἑαυτοῦ· πάντα γὰρ ταῦτα ταραχὰς ἐνποιεῖ τῇ φύσ[ει]. Bignone rightly compares it with fr. 3 of Democritus (taken from the π· εὐθυμίης): τὸν εὐθυμεῖσθαι μέλλοντα χρὴ μὴ πολλὰ πρήσσειν . . . , μηδὲ ἅσσ' ἂν πράσσῃ, ὑπέρ τε δύναμιν αἱρεῖσθαι τὴν ἑωυτοῦ καὶ φύσιν. Usener having already shown (*Rh. Mus.*, XLVII, 1892, p. 425) that the use of the word εὐθυμία, later abandoned by Epicurus, implies that this maxim belongs to a time when the Sage was still under the direct influence of Democritus (through Nausiphanes) and so probably to the time of the stay in Ionia, Bignone (*L'Arist. perd.*, II, pp. 217-19) has tried to refer this text to the letter of Epicurus 'to the philosophers in Mytilene' which dates, he says, from his stay in Lampsacus.

[32] Fr. 2 Us. The distinction is between pleasures 'at rest' (καταστηματικαὶ ἡδοναί) and pleasures 'in motion' (κατὰ κίνησιν), joy (χαρά) and a blossoming of the soul (εὐφροσύνη). According to Bignone, *L'Arist. perd.*, I, pp. 290ff, 321ff, Epicurus, in the remark from the π. αἱρέσεων καὶ φυγῶν quoted by Diogenes Laertius, X, 136, opposed his own idea of pleasure to that of the Cyrenaics (Aristippus). For the Cyrenaics ἀπονία is only a neutral state which cannot properly be called pleasure; real pleasure is of an active kind. Epicurus on the other hand, he says, gave the first place to the negative pleasures of ἀπονία and ἀταραξία which alone bring peace, whereas the pleasures 'in motion' imply intense activity (*intensa attività*, Bignone, p. 322) and a violent character (*quel carattere violento*, p. 323). Epicurus was led to oppose this by the fact that his antagonists (Heraclides of Pontus), reducing the εὐφροσύνη and χαρά here mentioned to the joy in feasting

of which Homer speaks (Od., IX, 5ff), asserted that Epicurus made this joy of the senses the τέλος of human life. It was to reject this interpretation that Epicurus opposed his idea of pleasure (καταστηματικαὶ ἡδοναί) to the joy and exhilaration (*esultanza*, p. 321) of the Cyrenaics, pleasures in movement which imply ἐνέργεια. At the same time he condemned Aristotelian εὐφρόσυνη which also is closely linked with ἐνέργεια. So argues Bignone.

I doubt whether it is necessary to detect a tone of disapproval in the use, in our text, of χαρά and εὐφρόσυνη. The evidence of Diog. Laert. is restricted to saying that as opposed to the Cyrenaics who admitted only pleasure 'in movement' Epicurus admitted the two kinds for the soul and the body (οἱ μὲν γὰρ τὴν καταστηματικὴν οὐκ ἐγκρίνουσι, μόνην δὲ τὴν ἐν κινήσει· ὁ δὲ ἀμφότερα ⟨τὰ γένη⟩ ψυχῆς καὶ σώματος) without showing any disapproval of the second kind. We have seen above (pp. 22-3) that he enjoined, and himself presided at, banquets between friends, at which he wished everyone to feast themselves (εὐωχεῖσθαι). Doubtless pleasure for him was a state of quietude, a serene disposition (γαληνισμός) which excludes all violent movement. But this state is not entirely negative, far from it, cf. fr. 68 Us.; 'The stability of a happy condition of the body (τὸ γὰρ εὐσταθὲς σαρκὸς κατάστημα) and the firm hope in the lasting nature of this condition allows a very deep and substantial joy (χαρά) to those capable of thought.' Better still, Epicurus himself distinguishes the negative state of *ataraxia* from the positive state of joy, cf. *Gn. V.*, lxxxi; 'Disturbance of the soul is not driven out, nor is true joy created by the possession of wealth, etc.' (οὐ λύει τὴν τῆς ψυχῆς ταραχὴν οὐδὲ τὴν ἀξιόλογον ἀπογεννᾷ χαρὰν οὔτε πλοῦτος κτλ.)

For χαρά, cf. again fr. 105 Us. = fr. 20 Bailey (a letter to Polyaenus which Usener suspects without reason); λέγε δή μοι, Πολύαιν', οἶσθ' ἅπερ ἡμῖν μεγάλη χαρὰ γεγένηται, and especially the letter from Epicurus to his mother *ap*. Diog. Oen., fr. lxiii W. (= 10 Us.) col. III-IV; πρὸς οὖν ταῦτα, ὦ μῆτερ, [θάρρει· οὐδὲν]γὰρ ἐπι[δηλοῖ σοι τὰ] φάσματα (!) ἡμ[ῶν κακόν]. τίθει δ'αὖ τ[οὐναντίον] καθ'ἡμέρα[ν χρήσιμ]όν τι ἡμᾶς π[αρακ]τωμένους εἰς [τὸ μακρ]οτέρω τῆς ε[ὐδαιμ]ονίας προβαίν[ειν· οὐ]γὰρ μεικρὰ οὐδέ[ν τ' ἰσχ]ύοντα περιγείνεται ἡ[μ]ε[ῖ]ν τάδ', οἷα τὴν διάθεσιν ἡμῶν ἰσόθεον ποιεῖ, καὶ οὐδὲ διὰ τὴν θνητότητα τῆς ἀφθάρτου καὶ μακαρίας φύσεως λειπομένους ἡμᾶς δείκνυσιν· ὅτε μὲν γὰρ ζῶμεν, ὁμοίως τοῖς θεοῖς χαίρομεν, fr. lxiv W. (= 11 Us.), col. I, l. 5; μετὰ δὴ τοιούτων ἡμᾶς ἀγαθῶν προσδόκα, μῆτερ, χαίροντας αἰεὶ καὶ ἔπαιρε σεαυτὴν ἐφ' οἷς πράττομεν. In a word, 'catastematic' pleasure is certainly characterized by the absence of pain and disturbance but it implies a positive joy which is not unaccompanied by spiritual activity, cf. again Cic., *Tusc.*, III, 18, 41 = fr. 67, p. 120, ll. 24-6 Us.; *laetantem enim mentem ita novi: spe eorum omnium quae supra dixi* (pleasures of the senses of sight and hearing), *fore ut natura iis potiens dolore careat.* Furthermore, as early as 1904, in his excellent work on *The Theory of Pleasure in Epicurus* (which Bignone does not seem to know), V. Brochard showed that εὐσταθεία σαρκός (fr. 8, p. 95, l. 10 Us., fr. 424, cf. fr. 68) which results at once from the removal of pain is a positive state. 'Pleasure is always produced when pain is removed. The removal of pain is a necessary and adequate condition for it but in itself it is perfectly positive and real. It is that physical well-being which results naturally from the equilibrium of the body or from health, it is the feeling itself of health or of life', *Etudes de phil. ancienne et de phil. moderne*, 2nd edn. (Paris, 1926), pp. 271-2; see also pp. 269ff.

[33] ἡ φυσιολογία in the terminology of Epicurus.

[34] *Ep.* III, 122. Cf. Ep. I, 37: 'Since I urge others to occupy themselves constantly in the study of nature and besides find in it that which brings the most peace into life' (καὶ τοιούτῳ μάλιστα ἐγγαληνίζων τῷ βίῳ, cf. I, 83 *end* τὰ κυρι-

ώτατα πρὸς γαληνισμόν). See also *Gn. V.*, x (Metrodorus) and Lucr., I, 72ff, III, 28ff.

[35] μελετᾶν, *ib.*, 122, μελέτα, 135.

[36] Cic., *De fin.*, I, 27, 71ff=fr. 227 Us.

[37] αἱ τῶν μετεώρων ὑποψίαι, *k.d.*, xi, cf. ὑποπτευόμενόν τι τῶν κατὰ τοὺς μύθους, *k.d.*, xii, τῶν ἄνωθεν ὑπόπτων καθεστώτων, *k.d.*, xiii. As long as φυσιολογία has not brought us certainty concerning celestial phenomena we are reduced to regarding them as the effects of arbitrary action by the gods; hence the fears and 'suspicions' which these phenomena inspire in us. To ὑποψία is opposed ἀσφάλεια, cf. *k.d.*, xiii, *Gn. V.*, xxxi πρὸς μὲν τἄλλα δυνατὸν ἀσφάλειαν πορίσασθαι, or, more exactly still, πίστις βέβαιος, *Ep.*, II, 85.

[38] μή ποτε πρὸς ἡμᾶς ᾖ τι; a typical expression, cf. *k.d.*, ii, ὁ θάνατος οὐδὲν πρὸς ἡμᾶς.

[39] For τῶν ἄνωθεν καὶ τῶν ὑπο γῆς, cf. Plato, *Theaetetus*, 173e ἡ δὲ διάνοια . . . πανταχῇ πέτεται κατὰ Πίνδαρον 'τά τε γᾶς ὑπενερθε' καὶ τὰ ἐπίπεδα γεωμετροῦσα, 'οὐρανόν θ'ὕπερ' ἀστρονομοῦσα, Hippocr., π. ἀρχ. ἰητρ. 1 (p. 36, 18 Heiberg) οἷον περὶ τῶν μετεώρων ἢ τῶν ὑπὸ γῆν.

[40] καὶ τὸ μακάριον ἐν τῇ περὶ μετεώρων γνώσει ἐνταῦθα πεπτωκέναι καὶ ἐν τῷ τίνες φύσεις αἱ θεωρούμεναι κατὰ τὰ μετεώρα ταυτί καὶ (s.e. ⟨τίνα⟩) ὅσα συγγενῆ πρὸς τὴν εἰς τοῦτο ἀκρίβειαν, *Ep.* I, 78. Usener wrongly excludes ἐν τῇ . . . γνώσει as a gloss on ἐνταῦθα. The meaning is not, 'Happiness lies in this, i.e. in the knowledge of τὰ μετέωρα', but, 'The happiness which the knowledge of τὰ μετέωρα brings lies in this, i.e. in the exact determination of the cause of τὰ κυριώτατα'. (In the same sense, Bignone, *L'Aristotele perduto:*, II, pp. 371-2 and 372, n. 1.) Construe καὶ ἐν τῷ τίνα ὅσα συγγενῆ with an ellipse of ἐστι after τίνα and ὅσα. Retain (with Bignone and Bailey) συγγενῆ (συντείνει Usener) and construe ὅσα συγγενῆ πρὸς ('relating to') τὴν ἀκρίβειαν εἰς τοῦτο (=εἰς τὸ μακάριον).

[41] Bignone, *L'Arist. perd.*, II, pp. 1-40 has firmly established this point.

[42] Cf. the texts of Seneca (*Ep.* 88, 42) and Philodemus (*Voll. Rhett.*, II, pp. 50ff Sudhaus), quoted by Bignone, *op. cit.*, II, pp. 65ff, 88ff. See also fr. 227 Us.

[43] Cf. *Ep.*, III, 122 οὔτε γὰρ ἄωρος οὐδείς ἐστιν οὔτε πάρωρος πρὸς τὸ κατὰ ψυχὴν ὑγιαῖνον, *Gn. V.*, liv οὐ προσποιεῖσθαι δεῖ φιλοσοφεῖν ἀλλ'ὄντως φιλοσοφεῖν· οὐ γὰρ προσδεόμεθα τοῦ δοκεῖν ὑγιαίνειν, ἀλλα τοῦ κατ' ἀλήθειαν ὑγιαίνειν. From these texts comes the equation, 'philosophy=to take care of the health of the soul'. Thus after a long detour we return to the pure Socratic doctrine, ἐπιμελεῖσθαι τῆς ψυχῆς ὅπως ὅτι φρονιμωτάτη καὶ βελτίστη ἔσται, cf. *Apol.* 29 e 1 and the note of Burnet *ad loc.* (Oxford, 1942).

[44] Friendship is the immortal good, at least according to Cicero, *De Fin.*, II, 25, 80 (quoted by Bignone, *ad loc.*): *praecepta quae didicisti . . . funditus evertunt amicitiam, quamvis eam Epicurus, ut facit, in caelum efferat laudibus.* Likewise Bailey, who compares *Ep.* III, 135, 7 οὐθὲν γὰρ ἔοικε θνητῷ ȝῴῳ ȝῶν ἄνθρωπος ἐν ἀθανατοῖς ἀγαθοῖς: friendship is an immortal good in the sense that it bestows a happiness similar to that enjoyed by the immortal gods. *Contra*, Usener, *art. cit.*, p. 305, and Diano, p. 148.

[45] Retain (with Bignone and Bailey) Φιλία (φιλοσοφία Hartel, Ἡλίου σφαῖρα ci. Usener) and μακαρισμόν (μακάριον βίον Weil). The whole sentence is full of reminiscences of the language peculiar to Greek mysticism. On the imagery of the herald (κηρύττουσα) and waking up (ἐγείρεσθαι), cf. *Corp. Herm.*, I, 26-8, IV, 3-4, VII, and my article in *Harv. Th. Rev.*, XXXI (1938), pp. 1ff. Μακαρισμός implies the notion of salvation. The friends of Epicurus are congratulated on having been saved just as the new initiates are congratulated in the Mysteries. Cf. Firm.

Mat., *De err. pr. r.*, 19,1 ⟨δι⟩ δε νύμφε, χαῖρε νύμφε, χαῖρε νέον φῶς: a formula used in the Mysteries of Mithras (cf. F. Cumont, *CRAI*, 1934, pp. 107-8; G. Heuten, ed. of *De err. pr. r.*, Brussels, 1938, p. 179; F. Cumont-M. Rostovtzeff, *Excav. at Doura Europos*, VII, 1939, p. 123; Corn, I. M. I. von Beek, *Pisciculi*, Munster, 1939, p. 42), but probably older. *Ib.*, 22, 1 (Mysteries of Osiris, of Attis, or of Adonis) θαρρεῖτε μύσται, τοῦ θεοῦ σεσωμένου· | ἔσται γὰρ ἡμῖν ἐκ πόνου σωτηρία. Apuleius, *Metam.*, XI, 22, p. 284, 7 Helm (the priest to Lucius, on the day of his initiation), *o Luci, te felicem, te beatum, quem propitia voluntate numen augustum tantopere dignatur; . . . adest tibi dies votis adsiduis exoptatus. Ib.*, XI, 24, p. 286, 5 H. *sic ad instar Solis exornato me et in vicem simulacri constituto, repente velis reductis, in aspectum populus errabat* (there follows the joyful feast of the *dies natalis*). Prudentius, *Peristeph.* 1046-8 (Mysteries of Attis after the taurobolium) *hunc inquinatum talibus contagiis,* | *tabo recentis sordidum piaculi,* | *omnes salutant atque adorant eminus* – Diels (*ad* Philod., *De dis*, I, p. 93, n. 1) has pointed out another borrowing by Epicurus and the Epicureans from the language of the Mysteries, τέλειος and its related terms. Cf. *Ep.* I, 36 ἐπεὶ καὶ τοῦ τετελεσιουργημένου τοῦτο κυριώτατον κτλ., *ib.*, 83 ὅσοι δὲ μὴ παντελῶς αὐτῶν τῶν ἀποτελουμένων (ἀποτετελειωμένων ci. Diels) εἰσίν, ἐκ τούτων κτλ. (*sic* Kochalsky, Diels, von der Muehll), Epic. *ap* Philod., *De dis*, I, p. 41, 10f. Diels τοῦ δ' ἄκρου λέγομεν ἀνθρώπου (sc. Epicurus) δεῖν ἀκούειν 'οὐδὲ τὸν τε[λείως] τέλειον οἱ θεοὶ πάντες ἅμα φοβεῖν γε νομίζονται', Philod., *De morte*, 34, 10 τῶν μὴ τελείων (as opposed to Socrates and the other matyr philosophers). We might add the famous saying of Metrodorus fr. 37 Körte (*Jahrb. f. class. Phil.*, Suppl. XVII, 1890) = *Gn. V.*, x = Clem. Al. *Strom.*, V, 138, p. 732P.: μέμνησο, Μενέστρατε, διότι θνητὸς φὺς καὶ λαβὼν βίον ὡρισμένον ἀναβὰς (Clem.: ἀνέβης *Gn. V.*) τῇ ψυχῇ ἕως ἐπὶ τὸν αἰῶνα καὶ τὴν ἀπειρίαν τών πραγμάτων κατεῖδες καὶ 'τά τ'ἐσσόμενα πρό τ'ἐόντα' (Hom., *Il.*, I, 70), where there is a mention of the theme of the ascent of the soul. If what follows, in Clement, is also from Metrodorus (*sic.* Zeller, III, 1, p. 456, n. 1, R. M. Jones, *Class. Philol.*, XXI, 1926, p. 113) we should see the language of the Mysteries in full use: ὅτε σὺν εὐδαίμονι χορῷ, κατὰ τὸν Πλάτωνα, μακαρίαν ὄψιν τε καὶ θέαν ἐποπτεύσομεν (ἐπωπτεύσαμεν Jones who cf. Plato, *Phaedrus*, 249c 2 ἅ ποτ' εἶδεν ἡμῶν ἡ ψυχή), . . . τελετήν . . . μακαριωτάτην τελούμενοι (cf. Phaedrus 249c, 8 τελέους ἀεὶ τελετὰς τελούμενος); but it is not certain that the quotation from Metrodorus goes beyond πρό τ'ἐόντα, and, even if it does, it may be nothing but a recollection from Plato. Note also Metrod. fr. 38 = Plut., *adv. Col.*, 17, p. 1117A: ποιήσωμέν τι καλόν ἐπὶ καλοῖς, μόνον οὐ καταδύντες ταῖς ὁμοιοπαθείαις (after being almost overwhelmed in emotions shared by all) καὶ ἀπαλλαγέντες ἐκ τοῦ χαμαὶ βίου εἰς τὰ 'Επικούρου ὡς ἀληθῶς θεόφαντα ὄργια.

[46] δεῖ μέντοι προκατάρχεσθαι. There is a hint of impatience in this μέντοι. No doubt Epicurus was reproached for giving too utilitarian a basis to friendship, just as he was reprimanded for reducing happiness to a ἡδονή of which the true meaning was misunderstood.

[47] ἐν τοῖς ταῖς ἡδοναῖς ἐκπεπληρωμ⟨ένοις⟩ Bignone: ἐκπεπληρῶν codd.

[48] Usener, *art. cit.*, p. 306, gives a bad translation, it seems to me, of οὔθ'ὁ μηδέποτε συνάπτων = 'noch wer Verpflichtungen meidet'. Epicurus is not opposing the man who seeks only his own interest to the man who never thinks of his friend's interest because these two attitudes are, in fact, the same. He is opposing completely interested friendship to friendship which is completely disinterested; the latter is just as blameworthy as the former because friendship implies that friends can be relied on. We meet again the thought of *Gn. V.*, xxiii and xxiv.

[49] A friend could only be brought to betray another by the fear of death or of an

evil of eternal or very long duration; but if no such evil exists he will never betray him. So friendship is perfectly secure. Bignone (*Epicuro*, pp. 21-3, 64, n. 6) and Bailey, *ad loc.*, have seen this point clearly. Retain τὴν . . . ἀσφάλειαν φιλίας (φιλίαις Usener, φιλίᾳ alii). Cf. *Life*, 120a 3 Bailey: the Sage τύχῃ τε ἀντιτάξεσθαι, φίλον τε οὐδένα προήσεσθαι ⟨καὶ ὑπὲρ φίλου ποτὲ τεθνήξεσθαι⟩. It seems obvious to me that these last words, out of place in Diog. Laert. (where they follow a remark on the behaviour of the Sage in sleep, 121b 9 Bailey) should be transposed to where I have put them.

[50] δεῖ δὲ καὶ παρακινδυνεῦσαι χάριν χάριν φιλίας Vat. is obviously a dittography and it is no help to appeal, with Bignone (*L'Ar. perd.* II, p. 300, n. 1), to *Gn. V.* ix κακὸν ἀνάγκη, ἀλλ' οὐδεμία ἀνάγκη ζῆν μετὰ ἀνάγκης, for if that maxim, which is well said though a little affected, makes sense, παρακινδυνεῦσαι χάριν χάριν φιλίας does not. Likewise Ed. Schwartz, *Charakterköpfe*, 112, p. 48 'aber man muss um eine Freundschaft zu gewinnen auch etwas riskieren'. P. von der Mühll retains the text (χάριν, χάριν φιλίας) and Diano defends it by making the first χάριν the subject of παρακινδυνεῦσαι.

[51] Cf. *k.d.*, xl: 'Those who have the power to make themselves completely secure as regards their neighbours' (ἐκ τῶν ὁμορούντων Bignone, *L'Ar. perd.*, II, p. 193, takes it as neuter, i.e. 'exterior circumstances' and cf. *Ep.*, II, 109, 12 τὰ ὁμοροῦντα. He also keeps the orthography of the mss., ὁμορρούντων, on account of *SIG*[3] 1044, 16 [Halicarnassus]), 'these also live a most pleasant life with one another because they possess the most solid guarantee for the future; and though they have enjoyed complete intimacy, if their friend dies before them' (or 'before the time' = προκαταστροφήν, 'a premature death' Bignone, Ernout, Bailey. I, however, prefer the other interpretation), 'they do not mourn for him as though they were lamenting his end'. See also fr. 186 Us. τῶν ἐσχάτων Νεοκλέους λόγων μεμνημένος ἐτήκετο τῇ μετὰ δακρύων ἰδιοτρόπῳ ἡδονῇ and on that Bignone, *L'Ar. perd.*, II, pp. 191ff.

[52] I have somewhat expanded the rendering of this maxim which has been taken from a more complete fragment on friendship and remains vague; καλλίστη καὶ ἡ τῶν πλησίον ὄψις, τῆς πρώτης συγγενείας ὁμονοούσης, ἢ [εἰ, secl. Bailey] πολλὴν εἰς τοῦτο ποιουμένη σπουδήν. True friendship is not based on ties of blood, but if to natural kinship is added a kinship of the spirit the sight of our relatives brings us 'to this' (εἰς τοῦτο), that is, without doubt, to a union still more intimate. On the incitement of ὄψις Bailey cites *Gn. V.*, xviii ἀφαιρουμένης προσόψεως καὶ ὁμιλίας καὶ συναναστροφῆς ἐκλύεται τὸ ἐρωτικὸν πάθος: see also the remark of Epicurus to Pythocles (fr. 165 Us.) quoted *supra.*, p. 40. Epicurus dearly loved his three brothers (ἥ τε πρὸς τοὺς γονέας εὐχαριστία καὶ ἡ πρὸς τοὺς ἀδελφοὺς εὐποιία *Life*, 10) who, on his advice, devoted themselves to wisdom (συνεφιλοσόφουν δ' αὐτῷ προτρεψαμένῳ καὶ οἱ ἀδελφοὶ τρεῖς ὄντες *Life*, 3). Cf. also Usener, *Epic.*, s.v. Νεοκλῆς.

[53] To which could be added others taken from the Epicurean school, e.g. Philod., *De dis*, III, p. 15, col. *c*, fr. 84 Diels: friendship exists also among the gods; without it their blessedness would not be complete (οὐκ ἂν ἦσαν τέλειοι κατ' εὐδαιμονίαν), cf. the comments of Diels, *Erläuterung*, pp. 6ff.

[54] Cf. for example the analysis of pleasure and pain in the *Philebus*, the description of certain moral virtues (especially in Bk. IV) and of friendship (Bks. VIII and IX) in the *Nichomachean Ethics*, and, in Epicurus, certain maxims on the genesis and nature of friendship.

[55] Cf. for example the remorse of Charisius when he realizes that having turned out his wife for misconduct he is just as guilty as she is, Menander, *Epitrepontes*,

693 (413)ff. The passage is all the more interesting because Charisius has been through the schools of wisdom; 'I the faultless, always worried about my reputation, *I who used to enquire ardently after what was good and what was bad*, I, the sage, upright and above reproach, now it's clear that I'm a man like all the others, etc.' In general the comedies of Menander are a good indication of the refinement of sentiment in this age.

[56] Not for the first time, of course, cf. my *Socrate* (Paris, 1934), *Contemplation . . . selon Platon*, pp. 69-73, and Ed. Des Places, *Socrate directeur de conscience* ap. *REG*, LI (1938), pp. 395-402, but we cannot say that this conception of the Sage was universal until Epicurus and the Stoics. On the Sage as 'spiritual director' in Roman times, cf. *Idéal*, pp. 73, n. 2; 74, n. 1 and 2.

[57] Cf. *Ib.*, p. 74, n. 2. Epicurus is called σωτήρ again in the letter from Plotina (wife of Trajan) to the Epicureans at Athens in 121, *SIG*[3], 834, 20 (cf. Diels, *Arch. Gesch. Phil.*, IV, 1891, pp. 486ff). See also Philod. *ap.* Pap. Herc., 346, 4, 19 ὑμνεῖν καὶ τὸν σωτῆρα τὸν ἡμέτερον (cf. Crönert, *Rh. Mus.*, LVI, 1901, p. 625), Luc., *Alex.*, 25, 61.

[58] Cf. the excellent article of A. D. Nock, *Conversion and Adolescence* ap. *Pisciculi*, pp. 165ff.

[59] ἐθηράθη, cf. Nock, *loc. cit.*, n. 11, 12, 13.

[60] Diog. Laert., IV, 16. According to Wilamowitz, *Antigonos von Karystos*, pp. 55-6, this story does not go back to Antigonus but to an unknown writer.

[61] ὥστε ποτὲ μελετῶν καὶ μεταξύ πως ἀποπαρδών, Diog. Laert., VI, 94.

[62] Crates the Cynic (4th century), not Crates the Academician, successor to Polemo as head of the Academy in 270.

[63] Cf. R. Herzog, *Philol.*, LXXXIX (1934), pp. 185-96, and before that Wilamowitz, *Der Menander von Kairo: N. Jahrb.*, XXI, 1908, p. 41, n. 1 (=*Kl. Schr.*, I, p. 258, n. 1). The boy has been converted by the Stoic philosopher Ariston. Wilamowitz compares and contrasts *Anth. Pal.* V, 134 (Posidippus).

[64] *Epicurea*, p. xlvi; *Kl. Schr.*, I, pp. 308-11. Usener notes in particular (with more or less certainty), *k.d.*, xxv, xxviii, *Gn. V.*, xvi, xviii, xxvi, xli, xliii, li, liii, lv, lxii, lxiii, lxv, lxvi, lxxi, lxxiii, lxxiv, lxxx. Add *k.d.*, xxiii and xxiv in view of the direct mode of address.

[65] *Gn. V.*, li, cf. *supra*, p. 29. Cf. *Gn. V*, lxxx: 'The first step to *salvation* (πρώτη σωτηρίας μοῖρα) is to watch over our own youth and to guard against everything that defiles us in the burning desires of the flesh.'

[66] καθὰ καὶ ὁ 'Επίκουρος [πικ]ρὰς [μέμψεις] πρὸς 'Απ[ολλ]ωνίδην ἐ[πό]ησεν, ὥστε καὶ τοι[αῦτ' αἰτι]ώμε[νος] . . . οἰκειῶσαι, fr. 118 Us. On this text, cf. the short note of K. Sudhaus, *Epikur als Beichtvater*, *ARW.*, XIV (1911), pp. 647-8.

[67] Fr. 176 Us., cf. Vogliano, pp. 49 and 116. Retain, with Vogliano, the vocative (.)ΑΠΙΑ (ἡ αἰτία Usener), but in this case I should think rather of a little boy (with a name of the type of Νικίας, etc.) in view of the injunction to obey *father* and Matro who must certainly be the παιδαγωγός (as Polyaenus for Pythocles) and a member of the Epicurean circle as well, cf. fr. 99 Us. Vogliano (p. 116) and after him Diano (p. 68, no. 163) withdraw the attribution of the letter to Epicurus and ascribe it to Polyaenus. According to Gomperz (first edn.) and Vogliano, we should read ΝΑΠΙΑ which Diano interprets as a boy's name, derived from νᾶπυ (cf. Ar., *Knights*, 631 κἄβλεψε νᾶπυ).

[68] Hermarchus was from Mytilene, Ctesippus perhaps from Mytilene or Lampsacus, Themista was the wife of Leonteus of Lampsacus, Pythocles perhaps either from Athens, where the name was very common, or from Lampsacus, where it occurred. His tutor Polyaenus was from Lampsacus: cf. *supra*, p. 20 and c. 2, n. 7.

69 He was not 18 when he came to the Master, Πυθοκλέους οὔπω γεγονότος ὀκτωκαίδεκα ἔτη, Plut., *adv. Colot.*, 29, p. 1124c (fr. 161 Us.).

70 Fr. 135 Us. εἰ βούλει πλούσιον Πυθοκλέα ποιῆσαι, μὴ χρημάτων προστίθει, τῆς δὲ ἐπιθυμίας ἀφαίρει. If we keep χρημάτων, which is well attested and besides recommended by the antithesis of the two genitives, we must regard it, with Bailey, as a partitive gen. (⟨τῶν⟩ χρημάτων would be more correct), cf. προκόπτειν τινὶ τῆς ἀρχῆς Thuc., IV, 60, ἐπιταχύνειν τῆς ὁδοῦ τοὺς σχολαίτερον προσιόντας Id., IV, 47. The opposition προστιθέναι—ἀφαιρεῖν is very common, Arist., *Eth. Nic.*, II, 4, 1106b, 11 τοῖς εὖ ἔχουσιν ἔργοις οὔτ' ἀφελεῖν ἔστιν οὔτε προσθεῖναι, Plato, *Cratylus*, 432a ἐάν τι ἀφέλωμεν ἢ προσθῶμεν, Thuc., V, 21 (of the treaty between Athens and Lacedaemon) ἢν δέ τι δοκῇ . . . προσθεῖναι καὶ ἀφελεῖν περὶ τῆς ξυμμαχίας. For the absolute use of the two verbs, cf. Arist., *Rhet.*, I, 4, 1359b, 28 οὐ γὰρ μόνον πρὸς τὰ ὑπάρχοντα προστιθέντες πλουσιώτεροι γίνονται, ἀλλὰ καὶ ἀφαιροῦντες τῶν δαπανημάτων, which presents also a parallel in thought.

71 Fr. 140*a*, p. 346, 2 Us. In the same way Crates the Cynic used to give his disciple Zeno the nick-name 'Phoinikidion', cf. Diog. Laert., VII, 3.

ss There is here, in Plutarch, a play on words which must have appeared before in the letter of Epicurus. The latter did not despise these verbal jests, e.g. *Gn. V.*, xxxiv οὐχ οὕτως χρείαν ἔχομεν τῆς χρείας παρὰ τῶν φίλων ὡς τῆς πίστεως τῆς περὶ τῆς χρείας.

73 καὶ πάσης τῆς . . . ἐπιλήψεως. The usual translation, 'acts of homage' (Bignone, Bailey), is much too weak. ἐπίληψις signifies the act whereby the worshipper takes hold of a limb of the adored one to kiss it; a concrete gesture, still to be seen in Mediterranean countries.

74 Cf. Xenoph., *Apol.*, 28 ἐπιθυμητὴς μὲν . . . ἰσχυρῶς αὐτοῦ (sc. Socrates), ἄλλως δ' εὐήθης. Cf. Burnet *ad* Plato, *Apol.*, 34a, 2; Kirchner, *Pros. Att.*, 1453 and *P.W.*, I, 2849, no. 15.

75 ἢ πάρει, Τιτάν, τὰ σκό[τη πά]ντα [ἐκ]δηλῶν p. 145 *adn.*, *ad.* l. 4 Usener. Τιτάν is one of the epithets of the Sun, *Hymn. orph.*, VIII, 2 Τιτάν χρυσαυγής, ὑπερίων, οὐράνιον φῶς, [Tib.], III, *Pan. Mess.*, 51, 114, 158. On Epicurus as = the Sun, cf. Lucr., III, 1042ff: *ipse Epicurus obit decurso lumine vitae,* | *qui genus humanum ingenio superavit et omnis* | *restinxit, stellas exortus ut aetherius sol* and *Idéal*, p. 74, n. 2.

76 ζήσεις δὲ ὡς θεὸς ἐν ἀνθρώποις, *Ep.*, III, 135, cf. *Gn. V.*, xxxiii.

77 Cf. Usener, *Kl. Schr.*, I, p. 309.

78 Cf. Cicero, *Tusc.*, I, 21, 48 *quae quidem cogitans soleo saepe mirari non nullorum insolentiam philosophorum, qui naturae cognitionem admirantur eiusque inventori et principi gratias exsultantes agunt eumque venerantur ut deum*, Pliny, *N.H.*, XXX, 5 *Epicurios voltus per cubicula gestant ac circumferunt secum* Cic., *de fin*, V, 1, 3 (*Epicuri*) *imaginem non modo in tabulis nostri familiares sed etiam in poculis et in anulis habent.*

79 The image is dear to Epicureans (v.g. Lucr., V, 11) and generally common in the Hellenistic Age, cf. *Idéal*, p. 124, n. 3.

80 *O apertam et simplicem et directam viam*, Cic., *de fin.*, I, 18, 57.

81 ἀφθάρτους καὶ ἰσοθέους ἀποκαλοῦντες αὐτούς, Plut., *c. Ep. beat.*, 7, p. 1091b.

82 Alexander, 25, 61.

## CHAPTER IV

### THE RELIGION OF EPICURUS

EVER since men in Greece had believed in the existence of gods – and this belief seems to go back to an unfathomable antiquity – they had thought also that the gods rule human affairs. These two aspects of faith are connected; for this very faith in the existence of superior powers, whose favour we must win and whose anger we must turn aside, is born of the observation, a thousand times repeated, that most of our actions do not achieve their object, that almost of necessity there remains a gap between our best laid plans and their fulfilment, and that as a result our being is circumscribed by doubt, whose offspring is hope and fear. By the same psychological law, human conjectures about the attitude of the gods varied according as men enjoyed prosperity or suffered misfortune. When our projects succeed we readily believe that the gods take notice of us, that they are good, and that they love us; but when we suffer a reverse, we imagine that the gods are far away, indifferent, or hostile. On this point Greek religion is no different from any other; it is one of the sentiments most deeply rooted in the heart of man and can be found alike in all peoples and in all times.

If there were any need to demonstrate the strength of these beliefs in Greece itself we should only have to dip into literature from the time of Homer.[1] Let me quote but one example, exactly contemporary with Epicurus. When in September 290 Demetrius Poliorcetes and his new wife Lanassa[2] made their solemn entry into Athens[3] as gods made manifest (Demetrius and Demeter), the city instituted a contest of paeans in honour of the divine couple. Now this is what we read in the paean of Hermocles, who carried off the prize:[4] 'As to him (Demetrius), he appears with a kindly face (ἱλαρός), as befits a god, and he is fair and full of joy . . . The other gods are far away, or they have no ears, or they do not exist, or they pay not the least attention to us: but you we see face to face, not in wood or in stone but in truth and reality.'[5] What could be more obvious? If the old gods are left on one side it is because they no longer concern themselves with the affairs of Athens and because for the last fifty years (since Chaeronea 338) Athens had lived under foreign domination. The gods of Athens are far away, or they have no ears: or even, since they are no longer active, they do not exist. Demetrius on the other hand appears as a smiling conqueror: it is he who is the god. Traditional expressions show how usual it was to link in this way the existence of the gods with their activity. A man could not succeed except 'with the gods' (σὺν θεῷ), he got nothing without them (οὐ θεῶν ἄτερ).[6] These expressions were so common that Epicurus did not hesitate to use them in his private letters. In the archonship of Charinus (308-7) he wrote to a friend: 'Even if war comes[7] it will bring us nothing dreadful if the gods are favourable (θεῶν εἵλεων ὄντων)', and again, 'Thanks to the gods (θεῶν εἵλεῶν ὄντων) I have lived and intend to live a pure[8] life in the company of Matro alone' (fr. 99 Us.).

As long as men ascribed to the gods the entire government of earthly matters they could not help but live in permanent anxiety. Theophrastus has given us a good example in his portrait, hardly overdrawn, of the *deisidaimōn*,[9] that is to say, not of the 'superstitious man' as it is usually translated,[10] but of the man who lives in perpetual fear of divine powers. 'Undoubtedly,' he begins, '*deisidaimonia* would seem to be a feeling of constant terror (δειλία) in regard to the divine power; and here is a picture of the *deisidaimōn*.' There follows a series of instances the accumulation of which certainly gives us the impression that such a man exaggerates, but each instance taken by itself shows nothing at all abnormal in Greek religion. Our *deisidaimōn* celebrates the Feast of Pitchers (16, 2); we shall soon see that Epicurus also took part in this feast without distinguishing himself in any way from the good people of Athens (τὴν τῶν Χοῶν ἑορτὴν συνεορτάζων, fr. 169 Us.). On the fourth and twenty-fourth days of the month, the *deisidaimōn* gives himself a holiday, has warm wine prepared, and spends his time garlanding the statues in his house (16, 10): Epicurus used to banquet with his friends on the twentieth day in each month.[11] Every month the *deisidaimōn* betakes himself with his children and his wife (or, in her place, the nurse) to the *Orpheotelestai* to renew his initiation (16, 11): we are told that Epicurus had himself initiated 'into the mysteries of the city – no doubt the Eleusinian mysteries – and into other (initiations?)'.[12] The *deisidaimōn* as such is distinguished by the keenness which makes him repeat the ceremony indefinitely, as though the first time did not afford him a sufficient guarantee. To shun the pollution brought by contact with a tombstone, a corpse, or a woman in childbed (16, 9) was, so to speak, one of the most rigid dogmas of Greek religion.[13] Equally there was nothing more common than the fear of bad omens (16, 3, 6, 8), the need to have an explanation of one's dreams (16, 11), the belief in the purificatory virtues of the olive (16, 2), of sea-water (16, 12), of garlic and the sea-leek (16, 13), the panic caused by the sight of a madman or an epileptic (16, 14),[14] or the veneration felt towards a snake that has glided into the house (16, 4). We must not, therefore, think that the *deisidaimōn* of Theophrastus is an exception: at the time of Epicurus, and much later still, he had thousands of brothers in all parts of the Greek world.[15]

It is clear, then, that for an infinite number of people religion remained a bondage which weighed heavily on their souls. No doubt in educated circles it was possible to banish the fear of the Olympians by denying their existence. It is also perfectly true that doubt and indifference as regards the civic gods had made great progress at the end of the fourth century; hence the parallel efforts on the one hand of Lycurgus and Demetrius of Phalerum to revive the official cults, on the other, earlier still, of Plato, of the author of the *Epinomis*, and of Aristotle (π. φιλοσοφίας) to introduce the new religion of the astral gods. But these well-educated men, more in the public eye perhaps and in any case better known to us because they were writers, are far from representing the masses. They remained attached to their gods, and so imprisoned in fear and hope; in fear, because they always had to dread that by an omission, even involuntary, of some ritual observation they might have offended the divinity; in hope, because it was always possible to believe that by purifications, sacrifices, and offerings the heart of the gods might be touched.

There is any amount of positive proof that these sentiments were thoroughly implanted in the pagan soul quite apart from the proof by implication provided by Lucretius' eloquent protest against the terrors of the over-devout. In the third century of our era one of the commonest motives for the popular hatred felt towards Christians was the belief that, neglecting the sacrifices themselves and encouraging others to do likewise, they had aroused the fury of the gods against the Empire. In 410, after the capture of Rome by Alaric and his Goths, this prejudice still had such power that St. Augustine was compelled to answer it; in the first ten books of the *City of God* he is engaged in showing that the Christians were not responsible for Rome's misfortunes.[16] Let us simply recall, to cut the matter short, Plutarch's little essay on *deisidaimonia*. Plutarch opposes atheism – by which he means the Epicurean doctrine[17] – to an excessive fear of the gods. But the latter evil seems to him worse than the former. Atheism may well be a false idea (ψευδὴς ἡ ὑπόληψις c.1., κρίσις οὖσα φαύλη c. 2), but at least it does not cause any unrest of soul; far from doing that, it steeps a man in a state of insensibility (εἰς ἀπάθειάν τινα δοκεῖ . . . περιφέρειν c.2) and as a result drives out fear (καὶ τέλος ἐστὶν . . . sc. τῇ ἀθεότητι . . . τὸ μὴ φοβεῖσθαι c.2). On the other hand *deisidaimonia* does untold harm. There is no peace any more for a man once he regards the gods as spiteful and given to doing harm (οἰόμενον μὲν εἶναι θεούς, εἶναι δὲ λυπηρούς καὶ βλαβεροῦς c.2); the Divinity is everywhere, it can pursue him even in sleep and beyond the grave.

No doubt not everything is original in this little work of Plutarch. Certain features were probably stock themes in the school of Epicurus since they are found both in Lucretius and Philodemus; Plutarch must have borrowed them from Epicurean literature.[18] Nevertheless when we read his finely drawn analyses we are very soon convinced that they are not merely a statement of commonplaces but are the result of observation and experience. Take for example chapter 7 where Plutarch is contrasting the feelings of the atheist and the *deisidaimōn* when things are not going as they would like (ἐν τοῖς ἀβουλήτοις). If the atheist is a moderate man he keeps silent and seeks his consolation within. If he has a peevish disposition he blames Chance or Fortune; accustomed to thinking that all is confusion here below, his own plight confirms him in that belief. In any event the atheist escapes more or less unharmed. It is otherwise with the *deisidaimōn*. 'If he suffers the most trivial misfortune he loses heart and builds upon his grief painful and serious afflictions from which he will be unable to rid himself; of his own accord he fills himself with fears and terrors, suspicions and worries, never ceasing to wail and groan. He blames neither man, nor chance, nor circumstances, nor himself but the sovereign Creator, God; it is from God, he would have us believe, that these tempestuous billows of heaven-sent malediction unfurl upon him. *According to him it is not because he is unfortunate but because the gods hate him that he is punished by them; that is why he submits to expiation and he is convinced that he deserves and has brought on himself everything he suffers.*'[19] This passage, and what follows, could have been written by the most modern spiritual director. The reason is that excessive fear of God is a malady which is always with us, and one of the most difficult to cure, as Plutarch notes. It is congenital with religious emotion and grows *pari passu* with that emotion because it is in proportion to the degree of faith. If we really believe that, giving no scope to secondary causes, God intervenes himself, directly, in the smallest incidents in our life, and if we are really conscious of the impurity of our being in comparison with the divine being, we are not far from being convinced that all our misfortunes have as their cause some sin or, more likely, that permanent state of sin which is the peculiar lot of man and which gives him his essential character in the eyes of God. Hence comes a continuous vexation of the Divinity because we never cease offending against him. 'How can one speak to the *deisidaimōn*? What means is there of helping him? He sits outside his house muffled in a miserable sack or girt in hideous rags. He often rolls naked in the mud *confessing at the top of his voice certain faults, certain omissions of which he is guilty,* crying out that he has drunk this and eaten that, or that he has followed such and such a course without the permission of his Guardian Spirit.'[20] Plutarch invents nothing; epigraphy confirms what he says. We possess such public confessions carved upon stone.[21]

This fear of the gods did not afflict men for this life only, it made them anticipate an eternity of punishment. No doubt generalization must be avoided, for the sentiments of the ancients on this subject admitted of infinite variation, especially perhaps in the Hellenistic age, from complete scepticism[22] to a sincere disquiet which drove a man to become initiated in all the oriental Mysteries so as to obtain a surer guarantee of immortality.[23] The belief in punishment beyond the grave had a long history in Greece, where the *Nekyia* of Homer, which all knew by heart,[24] had popularized it, and it appears in fourth-century literature. A client of Lysias declares herself ready to take the oath and, to give it more weight, recalls the punishments which are reserved in Hell for perjurors.[25] Cephalus, the father of Lysias, admits that ever since he became an old man he has been tormented by the fear of having to expiate in Hades the faults which he might have committed during his long life.[26] 'Demosthenes says that the author of a detestable law should be condemned to death so that he might administer his law to the impious in Hell. Elsewhere, he assumes that a base informer will one day be hurled by the infernal gods into the place where the impious are.'[27] The punishments of Hell were a favourite subject with painters; an archaic vase as early as the sixth century depicts them,[28] Polygnotus in the fifth had drawn them in the Lesche at Delphi, and a line from the *Captivi* of Plautus, a play imitated from a Greek original, is witness for the spread of these representations.[29] Finally, if the celebrated text in the *Republic* does not mean that a man could seek purification in the place of his dead parents so as to rescue them from their pains, it does at least prove that many had recourse to certain sacrifices in order to obtain pardon for their crimes both during life and also after death.[30]

So fear of the gods, fear of their anger towards the living and of their vengeance on the dead, played a great part in Greek religion. Perhaps Epicurus had experienced it himself. Perhaps he had undergone a crisis of conscience from which he had emerged victorious. If that is so we can understand better his unfailing certitude. He was convinced, at any rate, that *deisidaimonia* prevailed all about him, and as he had reached the haven of safety and, in a sentiment of universal benevolence,[31] wished to lead others into it, he felt it to be his first care to banish this fear which utterly prevents peace of mind (*ataraxia*).

Now the whole of this evil comes from a false notion about the gods. The remedy for the evil, that is to say, a true notion about the gods, will be furnished by the first principles themselves of the doctrine of *ataraxia*. The system of Epicurus is perfectly coherent on this subject, and the solution which it provides is not without elegance in its simplicity.

Freed from all anxiety by the limitation of his desires the Sage, in this world, finds peace of soul and thereby blessedness. But is it credible that the gods do not enjoy an equal happiness – the gods whom the Greek had always been accustomed to regard as immortal and happy beings par excellence[32] so much so that this double privilege of immortality and happiness is the very thing that essentially distinguishes the god from wretched, mortal man? Surely, if man can attain to happiness, so can the gods; and that which constitutes happiness for humans must also be the substance of the happiness enjoyed by the gods. Now human happiness consists of the absence of worry or, at least, this absence of worry is its first condition. It is to avoid being worried that a man restricts himself to the simplest mode of life, gives up the comforts of wealth, and lives apart from the world, politics, and affairs, thereby cutting off at the source all the causes of passion which might spoil his peace. The same considerations apply to the gods. It is absurd, then, to imagine that the gods constantly concern themselves with the government of the Universe and human affairs. That would run counter to the perfect serenity which is the basis of their happiness. 'Furthermore, we must not believe that the movement of the heavenly bodies, their turnings from one place to another, their eclipses, their risings and settings, and all such phenomena are brought about under the direction of a being who controls or will always control them[33] and who at the same time possesses perfect happiness together with immortality; for the turmoil of affairs, anxieties, and feelings of anger and benevolence do not go with happiness, but all that arises where there is weakness, fear and dependence on others' (*Ep.*, I, 76-77). 'Blessed and immortal Nature knows no trouble herself nor does she cause trouble to anyone else, so that she is not a prey to feelings either of anger or benevolence; for all such things only belong to what is weak' (*k.d.*, 1). 'In the first place believe that god is a living being, immortal and blessed, exactly resembling the common idea of the divine being that is engraved in us, and do not attribute to him anything that is alien to immortality or ill suited to blessedness, but consider that he possesses everything which can preserve his happiness and immortality. Certainly the gods exist – the knowledge that we have of them is clear vision[34] – but these gods are not as the vulgar believe them to be. For the vulgar do not know how to keep unblemished the idea they have of the gods.[35] And it is not the man who denies the gods of the vulgar who is impious, but he who attaches to the idea of god the false opinions of the vulgar. For the assertions of the vulgar about the gods are not concepts born of sensation (προλήψεις, cf. *Life*, 34), but erroneous suppositions. Hence it comes about that the worst injuries are inflicted on the wicked by the doing of the gods, as also the greatest benefits are conferred ⟨on the good⟩.[36] These latter, in fact, having through their own excellence been familiar during their whole life with the true nature of the gods gladly receive into their souls the gods who are like themselves, while they regard as foreign to the divine nature everything which is not such'[37] (*Ep.*, III, 123-124). 'From their indestructibility (i.e. the gods') it follows that they are strangers to all suffering; nothing can cause them any joy or inflict on them any suffering from outside' (fr. 99 Us. = Philod., π. εὐσ., p. 125 G.).[38]

In this situation, then, what was the religion of Epicurus likely to be? To begin with, there was no question of denying the gods: 'The gods exist, the knowledge which we have of them is clear vision'[39] (*Ep.*, III, 123). Far from reckoning Epicurus among the sceptics or the indifferent whose numbers were increasing at the end of the fourth century we must on the contrary regard him as one of those who reacted against the growing unbelief.[40] He himself believed in the gods and in the benefits of religion. He was punctilious in performing the traditional acts of worship and was, in short, a pious man in the sense in which the ancients understood that word.[41] That he must have received, in his childhood in Samos, the religious education of a young citizen of Athens goes without saying – even without giving currency to the story spread about by his enemies, 'that he used to go round with his mother from house to house so as to read the formulae for purification'.[42] Nor is it necessary, in order to be convinced of his piety, to note the use he makes of the language of the Mysteries,[43] for that might well be merely a literary borrowing.[44] It is enough to hear him speak: '⟨That the civic gods must be honoured⟩', declares Philodemus,[45] 'was not only the teaching of Epicurus but it is clear from his conduct also that he loyally observed all the traditional feasts and sacrifices. In the archonship of Aristonymus,[46] when writing to Phyrson about one of his fellow citizens, Theodotus, he says that he has joined in all the festivals . . . that he has celebrated with the people the festival of Pitchers (τῶν Χοῶν, on the 2nd day of Anthesteria) and has been initiated into the Mysteries of the city as well as other (initiations?).'[47] In another letter quoted by Philodemus,[48] Epicurus writes, 'As for us, let us piously and fittingly sacrifice on the proper days, and let us perform all the other[49] acts of worship according to custom, without letting ourselves be in any way troubled by common opinions in our judgments about the best and most august beings. Besides, let us remain also observant of custom for the reason I have mentioned;[50] for it is thus that we may live in conformity with nature . . .'[51] According to Philodemus again,[52] in the second book *On the kinds of Life* Epicurus says that the Sage 'will show marks of respect to the gods', and Philodemus adds a little later:[53] 'Furthermore it will appear that Epicurus loyally observed all the forms of worship and enjoined upon his friends to observe them, not only because of the laws but for reasons in conformity with the nature of things (διὰ φυσικὰς, sc. αἰτίας). Indeed, he says, in the book *On the kinds of Life*,[54] Prayer is proper to wisdom, not because the gods would be annoyed if we did not pray, but because we see how much the nature of the gods is superior to us in power and excellence.' Finally let me add the evidence of one of the ancients who was not a member of the School, Cicero, in his *De Natura Deorum*:[55] 'Certainly Epicurus holds that the gods exist and indeed I have never seen a man so afraid of things which, according to himself, he ought not to fear, I mean death and the gods.'

These texts are enough,[56] and there is not the least reason for interpreting the facts they report as evidence of hypocrisy. That charge is part of the usual collection of insults and calumnies that one sect hurled against another in antiquity. The Stoics used it against Epicurus and Plutarch repeats it after them.[57] Philodemus in turn throws it in the teeth of the Stoics.[58] In the same way, relying on the *De Mundo* which they wrongly attributed to him, the Fathers of the Church charged Aristotle with impiety,[59] and it is well known how often the crime of ἀθεότης has been imputed to the Christians. Such accusations, coupled most often with that of immorality,[60] are usually worthless. In the case of Epicurus it can be seen at once how easily they could arise from a misunderstanding of the Sage's thought.

Sincere in his fidelity to the civic cults Epicurus was not less so in the use he made in his writings of those interjections in which the name of the gods is called as witness. 'It would be laughable to mention that they sanctioned the use of oaths,' remarks Philodemus,[61] 'since their philosophic works are full of them.[62] It is right, however, to say that Epicurus urged them to keep the faith pledged by these and other oaths, and particucularly to respect the emphatic oath by the name of Zeus himself. For he is not the man to write, "In the name of . . . —but what shall I say? How can I speak piously?"[63] And he counsels Colotes to pay attention always to the regard for oaths and to the proper use of the name of the gods (καὶ πάσης θεολογίας).'

Epicurus, then, observed the forms of the State religion not only so as to 'obey the law' but from genuine feeling. Nevertheless his religion was not that of the common people. It differed from it in two ways.

In the first place, Epicurus' gods, being without cares like the Sage, take no interest in human affairs. Let us go over this essential dogma once again with the help of some quotations.[64] 'In his treatise *On Holiness* he (Epicurus) calls the life of the Divinity infinitely pleasant and happy, and he considers that we must remove all impurity from the notion we have about the divine, understanding[65] the conditions of such a kind of life (i.e.that of the gods) so that we adapt everything which happens to us to the manner of living which befits divine felicity. It is thus, thinks Epicurus, that holiness is made complete while at the same time common traditions are carefully preserved. But those people that we call "smitten with 'religious' dread", into what unsurpassable impiety do they not hurl themselves? He is not impious, who upholds the immortality and the supreme blessedness of God, together with all the privileges that we attach to those two. Rather he is pious who holds both opinions about the divine (i.e. that the divine is immortal and happy). And he who sees also that the good and ill sent us by God come without any unhealthy[66] anger or benevolence, shows clearly that God has no need of human things, but enjoys all good in full realization.' And again, 'Let it suffice to say now that the divine needs no mark of honour, but that it is natural for us to honour it, in particular by forming pious notions of it, and secondly by offering to each of the gods in turn the traditional sacrifices.'[67] '⟨If we admit that the gods take care of the world⟩ we must then admit[68] that they toil in an unsurpassable fashion, and not only for a limited time. For to say that we are convinced that the gods, being endowed with prudence, cannot enter into the category of bunglers, any more than zealous men here below, is, according to our doctrine, to destroy their serenity. Therefore to speak correctly we must assert that the gods know neither toil nor fatigue.'[69]

On the other hand, since the gods are indescribably happy, to praise them in prayer, to draw near to them on those solemn occasions when the city offers them a sacrifice, and to rejoice with them at the annual festivals is to take part in their happiness. That is why the disciple of Epicurus would be faithful to the prescriptions of religion. If the feasts at Athens were an occasion of merriment for all, the Epicurean had a still better reason for rejoicing. Was he not the equal of Zeus? As long as he suffered neither hunger nor thirst nor cold, as long as he was provided with a little barley-cake and water – easy things to obtain – he could rival Zeus himself in happiness.[70] That is why, also, the Epicurean sage did not scruple to call upon the name of the gods: 'He appeals to the Completely Happy so as to strengthen his own blessedness.'[71]

The Sage would perhaps have been surprised to hear it said, nevertheless it remains true that this religion of Epicurus is related to Plato's. Both put the goal of religious activity in the contemplation of beauty, and in so doing show themselves to be true sons of Greece.[72] For them, as for all Greeks, the divine being, whatever its essence, is a being of perfect beauty who lives a life of harmony and serenity.[73] Thus the Divine Universe of the *Timaeus* is a work of finished beauty which the Demiurge 'the best of artists',[74] has lovingly chiselled;[75] and this theme of beauty constantly recurs as the *leitmotiv* in every reference to the fabric of the Universe.[76] Likewise the gods of Epicurus are filled with beauty;[77] 'We must start from the nature of man so as to deduce, by analogy, the nature of the gods, and to assert, as a result, that the Divinity is a being living for ever and imperishable, and that it is totally filled with blessedness. Yet there is this reservation, that it does not admit of the fatigues of man or of the evils relating to death, to say nothing of the punishments after death, that we cannot attribute to it any of the things which make us suffer, but rather all good things, and that it possesses beauty in plenitude.' So again, following the Greek tradition,[78] the Divine Universe of the Timaeus is completely self-sufficient and needs nothing.[79] The same applies to the gods of Epicurus.[80] However, to quote from Plato,[81] these blessed gods who lack nothing 'have taken pity on the human race doomed by nature to suffer. They have therefore instituted, as moments of relief from our troubles, the festivals in which men hold converse with the gods, and they have given us as companions in the festivals the Muses, Apollo Musagetes, and Dionysus so that, associating with the gods in these meetings we might set right once again our way of living . . . Hence come rhythm and harmony. For the gods who have thus been given to us as companions in the dance make us feel pleasure when we perceive rhythm and harmony. It is they who, instructing us to move ourselves in order and making themselves our leaders, unite us one to another by a mixture of dances and songs and have called these exercises *choirs* (χορούς) from the joy which we feel in them (παρὰ τῆς χαρᾶς)'. Philodemus in his turn says,[82] 'It is principally through the gods that pleasure springs up in the heart of man (*voluptatem in homine a deo auctore creatam adserit principaliter*).' As Diels has well seen,[83] this remark refers to religious festivals. The gods have instituted these festivals to give us a share in their everlasting joy. No doubt a man can taste of the happiness of the gods at other times as well, whenever he receives into his soul the blessed emanations which flow from the persons of the gods.[84] But it is on festal days, when we approach the altar of sacrifice or contemplate the divine statue, that the influence of the gods makes itself more strongly felt and produces the greatest joy. 'That', says Epicurus, 'is the most essential thing and the one which is, as it were, pre-eminent. For every wise man has pure and holy opinions about Divinity and believes that its nature is noble and august. But it is particularly in festivals that he, progressing in the perception of its nature whilst having its name on his lips the whole time, comes by a more vivid sensation to understand (or, "to possess") the immortality of the gods.'[85] '⟨The Sage addresses prayers⟩[86] to the gods, he admires their nature and condition, he strives to come near to it, he aspires, so to speak, to touch and live with it, and he calls[87] wise men friends of the gods, and the gods friends of wise men.'[88]

All these elements of the Epicurean religion are brought together in a letter written by the Sage to an unknown friend;[89]

discovered in an Egyptian papyrus, recognized as belonging to Epicurus and carefully edited by Diels, this precious document will form a fitting conclusion to our analysis. In it we meet again, of course, the dogma of the *ataraxia* of the gods and, therefore, that of their indifference towards human affairs. But in it we see also that this dogma, far from abolishing religion, should purify it; the truly pious man does not approach the gods to appease them or to obtain some favour from them, but to unite himself to them by contemplation, to rejoice in their joy, and so to taste for himself, in this mortal life, their unending happiness.

'⟨It is no proof of piety to observe the customary religious obligations — though the offering of sacrifices⟩ on suitable occasions may be, as I have said, in keeping with nature — nor is it, by Zeus, when someone or other goes about repeating, "I fear all the gods, and honour them, and want to spend all my money in making sacrifices and consecrating offerings to them."[90] Such a man is perhaps more praiseworthy than other individuals,[91] but still it is not thus that a solid foundation for piety is laid. You, my friend, must know that the most blessed gift is to have a clear perception of things; that is absolutely the best thing that we can conceive of here below. Admire this clear apprehension of the spirit, revere this divine gift. After that, ⟨you should not honour the gods because you think thus to gain their favour⟩, as people will think when they see you performing acts of piety, but only because, in comparison with your own happiness, you see how the condition of the gods is infinitely more august, according to our doctrine. And certainly, by Zeus, ⟨when you practise⟩ this doctrine — the doctrine most worthy of belief, ⟨as your reason should tell you — it is of course open to you to offer sacrifices to the gods. By doing so you perform⟩ an act which gives confidence and is a pleasure to see, if it is done at the proper time, because you honour your own doctrine by enjoying those pleasures of the senses which befit such occasions and besides you conform in some sense to religious traditions. Only be careful that you do not permit any admixture of fear of the gods or of the supposition that in acting as you do you are winning the favour of the gods.

'For indeed, in the name of Zeus (as men affect to say) what have you to fear in this matter? Do you believe that the gods can do you harm? Is not that, on any showing, to belittle them? How then will you not regard the Divinity as a miserable creature if it appears inferior in comparison to yourself? Or will you rather be of the opinion that by sacrificing thousands of oxen you can appease God if you have committed some evil deed? Can you think that he will take account of the sacrifice and, like a man, remit at some time or another a part of the penalty?

'No doubt men tell each other that they should fear the gods and honour them with sacrifices so that, restrained by the tribute they receive, the gods will not attack them; as a result they think that if their surmise is correct they will altogether escape injury and if it is not, all will be well because they pay homage to the power of the gods. But if these close relations ⟨between gods and men were really to exist it would be a great misfortune, for the effect would make itself felt even beyond the grave⟩, after the funeral ceremonies, as soon as a man was cremated. For then men would suffer injury even beneath the earth and everyone would have to expect punishment. Moreover, I need not describe how men would have to beg for signs of favour from the gods in their fear of being neglected by them (for they would think to induce the gods in this way to communicate with them more readily and come down into their temples), any more than I can tell of the diversity and number of the methods they would employ because of their fear of harm and so as to guard against punishment. For to speak the truth all this seems a pure illusion of these people when compared with the doctrine of those who think that a life of happiness exists for us in this world and do not admit that the dead live again – a marvel not less unlikely than those which Plato imagined.'

## NOTES

[1] Cf. *La Sainteté*, chap. II, *Le Héros grec*, especially pp. 58ff.

[2] Daughter of Agathocles of Syracuse; married Pyrrhus as her first husband.

[3] Cf. the entry into Athens of Peisistratus accompanied by a beautiful young woman dressed as Athena, Aristotle, *Ath. Pol.*, XIV, 4.

[4] Cf. J. U. Powell, *Collectanea Alexandrina*, p. 173. On these events cf. W. W. Tarn, *Antigonos Gonatas* (Oxford, 1913), p. 49 and W. S. Ferguson, *Hellenistic Athens* (London, 1911), p. 143.

[5] The pun οὐδὲ λίθινον, ἀλλ' ἀληθίνον cannot be reproduced in French, or English. Note the iotacism.

[6] Cf. *Idéal*, pp. 24-5 with the notes.

[7] Epicurus was then living in Lampsacus, a town dependent on Lysimachus, the master of Thrace and the Hellespont (de Witt, *op. cit.*, pp. 78ff). It is not possible to say what war was threatening Lampsacus at the time, but as hostilities were almost continuous between Lysimachus and Antigonus for the possession of the straits, Epicurus is perhaps alluding to some incursion by Antigonus' fleet.

[8] καθαράν-pure, I think, of all vain anxiety.

[9] *Characters*, 16. Cf. the commentary of O. Navarre, Paris, 1924, and of H. Bolkenstein, *Theophrastos' Charakter der Deisidaimonia als religionsgeschichtliche Urkunde* (*RGVV*, XXI, 2, 1930).

[10] Our 'superstitious' is a less accurate rendering than *superstitiosus* of the real meaning of δεισιδαίμων, cf. Varro, fr. 29a, Agahd (Aug., *Civ. dei*, VI, 9): *cum religiosum a superstitioso ea distinctione discernat* (sc. Varro), *ut a superstitioso dicat* timeri *deos, a religioso autem tantum* vereri *ut parentes, non ut hostes timeri, atque omnes ita bonos dicat, ut facilius sit eos nocentibus parcere, quam laedere quemquam innocentem* . . . ; Serv., *in Aen.*, VI, 596: *religiosi sunt qui per reverentiam timent*, VIII, 187, *superstitio est timor superfluus atque delirus.* For the Roman, then, the *superstitiosus* was the devotee moved by scrupulous fear (of having angered the divinity), the *religiosus* (εὐλαβής) he who worshipped with a feeling of reverence. In his famous definition (*N.D.*, II, 28, 71-2), Cicero allows himself to be misled by a false etymology and obscures everything: *quos deos et venerari et colere debemus. Cultus autem deorum est optimus idemque castissimus atque sanctissimus plenissimusque pietatis, ut eos semper pura integra incorrupta et mente et voce veneremur. Non enim philosophi solum verum etiam majores nostri superstitionem a religione separaverunt: nam qui totos dies precabantur et immolabant, ut sibi sui liberi superstites essent, superstitiosi sunt appellati* . . . ; *qui autem omnia quae ad cultum deorum pertinerent diligent er retractarent et tanquam relegerent, i sunt dicti religiosi.*

[11] Cf. *supra*, p. 22, and c. II, n. 15.

[12] τὰ μυστήρια τὰ [ἀστι]κὰ καὶ τὰς ἄλλας[τελετὰς μυούμενος supplevi exempli gratia, p. 169 Us.

[13] Among many examples, cf. Theophr., *Characters*, 16, 9. See also my *Religion grecque* (*Histoire generale des Religions*, II, Paris, Quillet, 1944), pp. 54-7.

[14] Cf. Hippocr., π. ἱρῆς νόσου for the epileptic and, for the insane, e.g. Eurip., *Troades*, 169ff (Hecuba to the Chorus) μή νύν μοι τὰν | ἐκβακχεύουσαν Κασάνδραν | πέμψητ' ἔξω, | αἰσχύνην 'Αργείοισιν, | μαινάδ', ἐπ' ἄλγει δ' ἀλγυνθῶ.

[15] Speaking of the taste for tales of divine vengeance and punishments in many writings of Heraclides of Pontus, Bignone rightly observes that the popularity of these tales in the Hellenistic age shows how the old idea of *nemesis* still persisted; cf. *L'Ar. perd.*, I, pp. 282-4: 'Ma l'età ellenistica a torto si considera . . . eccessivamente scettica, mentre amava invece questi ritorni all'antico pietismo. Non aveva dunque del tutto torto Epicuro . . . di accusare di superstizione i filosofi della scuola platonico-peripatetica' (p. 284).

[16] Cf. the remark in *Civ. Dei*, II, 3: *pluvia defit, causa Christiani sunt.*

[17] Cf. ἀτόμους τις οἴεται καὶ κενὸν ἀρχὰς εἶναι τῶν ὅλων, c. 1. The charge of impiety was common against the Epicureans, cf. Usener, *Epicurea*, pp. lxxiff.

[18] So for example the idea that the gods pursue us even in Hades. Cf. Lucr., I,

110-11, *nunc ratio nullast restandi, nulla facultas,* | *aeternas quoniam poenas in morte timendumst.* Philod., *De dis,* I, col. XVII, 9ff (p. 29 D). ἀλλ' ε[ἰκὸς] τῶι μὲν ὑποστη[σαμέ]νωι | τοὺς θεοὺς ἐν τῷ ζῆν μόνον ἰλ[αστοὺς] | ἀργαλεωτέρ[αν] εἶναι τὴν περὶ τοῦ θανάτου ταραχὴν ὡς ἂν αἰωνίους ἐφ' αὐτῶι [συμ]φορὰς προβάλλοντι, col. XVIII, 1-3 (p. 30 D., cf. p. 77) ἐὰν ἐμβάλῃς Ἅδου πάλιν τὰ κ[οινῶς] ὑπ[ολ]ηφθέντα δ]ε[ιν'], ἀναπνεῖ[ν οὐ δύνανται] = 'If you throw once again into the hearts of men the terrifying notions the vulgar have about Hades, they can no longer breathe', although they must have realized that in death they will feel nothing any more (ἐπαισθήσεσθαι [τοὺς θανόντα]ς . . . μηδαμῶς, col. XVIII, 4-5). Plut., *De Superst.*, c. 3: For everyone sleep is a time of repose, but not for the *deisidaimōn*: μόνη γὰρ (ἡ δεισιδαιμονία) οὐ σπένδεται πρὸς τὸν ὕπνον, οὐδὲ τῇ ψυχῇ ποτε γοῦν δίδωσιν ἀναπνεῦσαι καὶ ἀναθαρρῆσαι, τὰς πικρὰς καὶ βαρείας περὶ θεοῦ δόξας ἀπωσαμένῃ (cf. Cic., *De Divin.*, II, 72, 150 *perfugium videtur omnium laborum et sollicitudinum esse somnus. at ex eo ipso plurimae curae metusque nascuntur; qui quidem ipsi per se minus valerent et magis contemnerentur, nisi somniorum patrocinium philosophi suscepissent*), c. 4: πέρας ἐστὶ τοῦ βίου πᾶσιν ἀνθρώποις ὁ θάνατος· τῆς δὲ δεισιδαιμονίας, οὐδ' οὗτος· ἀλλ' ὑπερβάλλει τοὺς ὅρους ἐπέκεινα τοῦ ζῆν, μακρότερον τοῦ βίου ποιοῦσα τὸν φόβον, καὶ συνάπτουσα τῷ θανάτῳ κακῶν ἐπίνοιαν ἀθανάτων.

[19] Based on Trad. Bétolaud (Paris, 1870).

[20] *Ib.*, c. 7, same translation.

[21] Cf. *Le Monde gréco-romain au temps de N.S.*, II, pp. 120-7, esp. pp. 124ff. Add the inscriptions in the sanctuary of Apollo Lairbenos in Phrygia, *MAMA*, IV (1933), nos. 279ff. (=*SEG*, VI, nos. 248ff) and cf., on these texts, A. Cameron, *Harv. Th. Rev.*, XXXII (1939), pp. 155ff.

[22] Callim., *Epigr.*, 13. Cf. *supra*, p. 12.

[23] On this diversity see the accurate comments of H. Weil in his review of Rhode's *Psyche, Etudes sur l'antiquité grecque* (Paris, 1900), pp. 85-6. Some of the references which follow are borrowed from this article, pp. 82-4.

[24] Cf. especially A. Dieterich, *Nekyia*, 2nd edn., Leipzig-Berlin, 1913.

[25] Lys., *c. Diogiton*, 13.

[26] Plato, *Rep.*, I, 330d-1b.

[27] Weil, *loc. cit.*, p. 83, quoting Demos., *Timocrates*, 104 and *Aristogiton*, I, 53.

[28] An archaic vase from Palermo, cf. G. Méautis, *L'Ame hellénique d'apres les vases grecs* (Paris, 1932), figs. 44 and 45.

[29] Plautus, *Captivi*, V, 4, 1 *vidi ego multa saepe picta, quae Acherunti fierent* | *cruciamenta.*

[30] This is how, with H. Weil (*loc. cit.*, p. 85) and others, I understand ὡς ἄρα λύσεις τε καὶ καθαρμοὶ ἀδικημάτων διὰ θυσιῶν καὶ παιδιᾶς ἡδονῶν εἰσὶ μὲν ἔτι ζῶσιν εἰσὶ δὲ καὶ τελευτήσασιν. 'They (the *Orpheotelestai*) can bring it about that the wicked are not punished by the gods, either in this life or after death' (Weil).

[31] καθόλου τε ἡ πρὸς πάντας αὐτοῦ φιλανθρωπία, *Life*, 10.

[32] Cf. *Idéal*, pp. 23-5 and Epicurus, *Ep.*, I, 76 καὶ ἅμα τὴν πᾶσαν μακαριότητα ἔχοντος μετὰ ἀφθαρσίας, III, 123 πρῶτον μὲν τὸν θεὸν ζῷον ἄφθαρτον καὶ μακάριον νομίζων, *k.d.*, i τὸ μακάριον καὶ ἄφθαρτον.

[33] The better MSS. have διατάξοντος, three (GHZ), διατάξαντος adopted by Bailey alone. The difficulty lies in the disjunctive ἢ (διατάττοντος ἢ διατάξοντος). According to Bailey (p. 250), Epicurus is distinguishing between a God who regulates indefinitely the celestial movements and a God who, at the Creation, has regulated them once for all so that they go on automatically; hence his choice of διατάξαντος. Von der Muehll refers to *k.d.*, xvi; the λογισμός of the Sage has ordered, orders,

and always will order (διῴκηκε . . . καὶ διοικεῖ καὶ διοικήσει) the greatest and most important things in his life; but there the text has καί and not ἤ. Bignone (*L'ar. perd.*, II, pp. 376-8) thinks that Epicurus is alluding to the myth in the *Politicus* (269c) where God sometimes regulates personally the movement of the Universe and sometimes leaves it to itself, so that it returns to its congenital disorder. I doubt whether ἤ has here the force of an absolute disjunctive, 'either . . . or else'. The idea is, 'We must drive out the notion of a god who regulates or will continue indefinitely to regulate the movements of the heavens'; neither now nor at any time in the future will God govern the world, so we need not disturb ourselves.

34 On the word ἐναργής which is a technical term in Epicurus, cf. *infra*, note 39.

35 While thinking of the gods as immortal and blessed, the vulgar ascribe to them passions which contradict that double privilege, cf. Bignone and Bailey, *ad loc.*

36 The addition ⟨τοῖς ἀγαθοῖς⟩ by Gassendi is indispensable. 'Good' and 'wicked' are opposed here like 'wise' and 'foolish', cf. Philod., *De dis*, I, col. XII, 17ff (p. 20 D.) ὁ δ' Ἐπίκουρος ἀνδρὰς ἀ[γαθοὺ]ς ἐκώλυε νοεῖν τοιαῦτα οἷ'ἂν ἐκ[βάλλῃ τὸ] εὐδοκῆσαι.

37 ἔνθεν αἱ μέγισται βλάβαι τε τοῖς κακοῖς ἐκ θεῶν ἐπάγονται καὶ ὠφέλειαι ⟨τοῖς ἀγαθοῖς⟩. ταῖς γὰρ ἰδίαις οἰκειούμενοι διὰ παντὸς ἀρεταῖς τοὺς ὁμοίους ἀποδέχονται, πᾶν τὸ μὴ τοιοῦτον ὡς ἀλλότριον νομίζοντες. For this difficult passage (place a full-stop before ἔνθεν), I have adopted, after reflexion, the sense proposed by Usener (who, *Epic.*, pp. xx-xxi, refers to fr. 385, to Lucr., VI, 68ff and to Philod., π. εὐσ., p. 86, 13 G.) and by Bignone. Bailey's objections (pp. 330-1) do not seem to me to be sound. ἔνθεν is not a useless repetition of ἐκ θεῶν but refers to the whole of the preceding clause. It does not say that the gods cause harm to the wicked (Bailey asks: 'Is there any evidence in Epicureanism for the idea that the images of the gods do harm to the evil?'), the wicked injure themselves by their false conception of the gods, as the good derive benefit from their correct notions because they are thereby allowed to share in the *ataraxia* of the gods.— In spite of *Ep.*, I, 37 τοῖς ᾠκειωμένοις φυσιολογίᾳ ('for those who are used to the study of nature'), I believe that ταῖς γὰρ ἰδίαις οἰκειούμενοι ἀρεταῖς means here not 'used to their own virtues' ('adusati alle proprie virtu' Bignone, 'being accustomed to their own virtues' Bailey), but 'made familiar with the gods through their own virtues' (as already suggested by Ernout who perhaps strains the meaning: 'the latter are made completely akin to the gods by their own virtues'). Further, ἀρεταί here has not so much the sense of 'moral virtues' as that of 'excellence' (i.e. the condition of *ataraxia* which assimilates the Sage to God).

38 A letter of Epicurus to an unknown friend written in the archonship of Charinus (308/7).

39 ἐναργής 'clear to the eyes' (of the body or the soul) means in Epicurus that which is seen by direct intuition and is therefore obvious. Our knowledge of the gods comes by a kind of immediate vision in the sense that subtle images flow from their persons, imprint themselves directly on our minds, and there create the 'universal concept' (ἡ κοινὴ νόησις) of god, cf. Bailey, *ad* III, 123 and pp. 259ff, especially pp. 264-7. With ἐναργὴς γὰρ αὐτῶν ἡ γνῶσις. cf. Plato, *Theaet.*, 206b, 7 πολὺ τὸ τῶν στοιχείων γένος ἐναργεστέραν τε τὴν γνῶσιν ἔχειν φήσομεν καὶ κυριωτέραν τῆς συλλαβῆς πρὸς τὸ λαβεῖν τελέως ἕκαστον μάθημα. For ἐναργής, cf. fr. 255 Us. πρόληψιν δὲ ἀποδίδωσιν (sc. Epicurus) ἐπιβολὴν ἐπί τι ἐναργὲς καὶ ἐπὶ τὴν ἐναργῆ τοῦ πράγματος ἐπίνοιαν, Epic., π. φύσεως, κ'η', fr. 5, col. VII, 10 inf. (p. 14 Vogl.) ὁ δὲ ἐπιλογισμὸς εἰς γνῶσιν τῶν ἀφανῶν κέχρηται τ[ῆι ἐναρ]γεῖ κτήσει, *ib.*, fr. 5, col. XI, 6 (p. 18 Vogl.). For ἐνάργημα (? coined by Epicurus),

cf. *Ep.*, I, 72: we must not judge time by referring it to a concept which we perceive in our own minds, ἀλλ' αὐτὸ τὸ ἐνάργημα (the direct intuition) . . . ἀναλογιστέον, *Ep.*, II, 91: the real size of the stars is as it appears to our eyes, every objection on this point vanishes ἐάν τις τοῖς ἐναργήμασι προσέχῃ, ὅπερ ἐν τοῖς περὶ φύσεως βιβλίοις δείκνυμεν, II, 93: πάντα γὰρ τὰ τοιαῦτα (all these kinds of explanation) . . . οὐθενὶ τῶν ἐναργημάτων διαφωνεῖ, II, 96: ἐπὶ πάντων γὰρ τῶν μετεώρων τὴν τοιαύτην ἰχνεύειν οὐ προετέον. ἢν γάρ τις ᾖ μαχόμενος τοῖς ἐναργήμασιν, ουδέποτε μὴ δυνήσεται ἀταραξίας γνησίου μεταλαβεῖν. ἐνάργημα is then the element of self-evidence which must prevail and serve as a criterion. For ἐνάργεια (already used by Plato in *Polit.*, 277c 3, where Plato compares his discourse to a painting already finished in its general outlines but still lacking the ἐνάργεια – the preciseness and boldness given by the harmony of colours), cf. *Ep.*, I, 48: οὐδὲν γὰρ τούτων (i.e. of this doctrine) ἀντιμαρτυρεῖται ταῖς αἰσθήσεσιν, ἂν βλέπῃ τις τίνα τρόπον τὰς ἐναργείας (the clear vision of external objects), τίνα καὶ τὰς συμπαθείας ἀπὸ τῶν ἔξωθεν πρὸς ἡμᾶς ἀνοίσει (sc. ἡ αἴσθησις), I, 52: καὶ ταύτην οὖν σφόδρα γε δεῖ τὴν δόξαν κατέχειν, ἵνα μήτε τὰ κριτήρια ἀναιρῆται τὰ κατὰ τὰς ἐναργείας (the criteria based on self-evidence), I, 71: καὶ οὐκ ἐξελατέον ἐκ τοῦ ὄντος ταύτην τὴν ἐνάργειαν (we must not exclude from the realm of Being the element of self-evidence that is constituted by accidentals and sensible objects apprehended conjointly), I, 82: ὅθεν . . . προσεκτέον . . . ταῖς αἰσθήσεσι, . . . καὶ πάσῃ τῇ παρούσῃ καθ' ἕκαστον τῶν κριτηρίων ἐναργείᾳ (we must remain attentive to the elements of self-evidence in conformity with each of the criteria), *k.d.*, xxii: τὸ ὑφεστηκὸς δεῖ τέλος ἐπιλογίζεσθαι καὶ πᾶσαν τὴν ἐνάργειαν, ἐφ' ἣν τὰ δοξαζόμενα ἀνάγομεν (we must always consider the actual purpose and the whole collection of the elements of self-evidence to which we refer our judgments, – without which there will be nothing but doubt and confusion).

[40] Bignone, *L'Ar. perd.*, II, pp. 367ff, has brought this point out well.

[41] He had written a περὶ ὁσιότητος, cf. *Life*, 27 (end), Usener, *Epicur.*, pp. 106-8, and a περὶ εὐσεβείας, Usener, p. 100.

[42] *Life*, 4, in a passage where Diogenes Laertius retails some of the slanders put out against Epicurus. This is a commonplace (cf. Demos., *De Cor.*, 258), and Bignone (*L'Ar. perd.*, II, p. 367) is wrong, in my opinion, to regard it as authentic fact.

[43] So Bignone, *op. cit.*, II, p. 369, referring to Diels *ad* Philod. *De dis*, I, p. 93, n. 1: cf. *supra*, c. III, n. 45.

[44] Already met with in Plato. Cf. *Idéal*, pp. 116ff (*Mystères cultuels et mystères littéraires*).

[45] Philod., π. εὐσ., p. 127 G. = fr. 169 Us. See also the passages from bk. II of the π. εὐσ. reconstructed by Philippson, *Hermes*, LVI, pp. 364ff, especially pp. 366-7, 372-3 and 379.

[46] Perhaps 289/8: cf. *P.W.*, s.v., no. 7.

[47] τὴν τ[ῶν] Χοῶν ἑορτὴν [συν]εορτάζων καὶ [τὰ] μυστήρια τὰ [ἀστι]κὰ (Usener: ['Αττι]κὰ Gomperz) καὶ τὰς ἄλλας [τελετὰς μυούμενος supplevi]. Cf. fr. 157 Us. = Philod., π. εὐσ., p. 105 G. (a letter of Epicurus to Polyaenus): [συνεορτασ]τέα κἂν ['Ανθεστήρι]α, καὶ γὰρ το[ῦ θείου] ἐπιμνηστέ[ον]. But Usener admits: 'Lusi quae proposui', p. 149, *ad.* l. 13. Philippson, *Hermes*, LVI, 373, reads: [συνεορτασ]τέα κ' 'Αν[θεστήρι]α· καὶ γὰρ τῶ[ν θεῶν] ἐπιμνηστέ[ον ὡς αἰ]τίων πολλῶν [ἀγαθῶν ὄντω]ν.

[48] Philod., π. εὐσ., p. 126 G. = fr. 387 Us., cf. Diels, *Sitz. Ber. Berlin*, 1916, p. 896.

[49] κα[ὶ τ]ἄλλα πάντα πράττωμεν Gomperz, Usener, Diels: κα[ὶ κ]αλῶ[ς] π. πράττωμεν Bailey (fr. 57).

[50] ἔτι δὲ καὶ δίκαιο[ι ὦ]μεν ἀφ' ἧς ἔλε[γον δό]ξης, cf. fr. 13 Us. οὐ μόνον [διὰ

τ]οὺς νόμους, ἀλλὰ διὰ φυσικὰς [αἰτίας]. Diels reads: ἔτι δὲ καὶ δίκαιό[ν φα]μεν ἀφ' ἧς ἔλε[γον δό]ξης 'Moreover we pronounce that it is just for the reason I have given'.

[51] The rest is too mutilated to make sense. Diels completes it thus οὕτωι (!) γὰρ [ἐν]δέχεται φύσι[ν θνη]τὴν ὁμοίω[ς Δι]ὶ νὴ Δία ȝῆν, [ὡς φαί]νεται· κἀν [τῶι Πε]ρὶ βίων δὲ π[ερὶ τῆς προσκυνή]σεως . . . i.e. 'for it is thus that the mortal nature, by Zeus, is permitted to live like Zeus, as it appears. And in his treatise *On the Kinds of Life*, about marks of adoration. . . .'

[52] Philod., π. εὐσ., p. 126, 26 G.=fr. 12 Us.

[53] *Ib.*, p. 128, 5 G.=fr. 13 Us.

[54] ἐν τῶι Περὶ [βίων] Usener: Περὶ [θεῶν] Buecheler, perhaps more correctly.

[55] Cic., *N.D.*, I, 31, 86. Cotta is speaking.

[56] Without even mentioning the private cults of the sect, on which cf. *supra* c. II, n. 14. The text from Philod., π. εὐσ., p. 104 G. is read by Diels (*loc. cit.*, p. 894) as follows: παραγίνεσθαι ἀλ]ηλιμμένον [ἐπὶ δεῖπν]ον, αὐτόν τε [ἑορτὴν τ]αύτην ἄγειν [τὴν ταῖς] εἰκα⟨σ⟩ι διαφό[ροις εἰλ]απινα⟨σ⟩ταῖς [ἀξίως] τὴν οἰκίαν ὀ[πώραις] ἐπιλαμπρύ[ναντά τ]ε καὶ καλέσαν[τα πάν]τας εὐωχῆσαι i.e. '(Epicurus was accustomed) to come to the banquet anointed with oil and to celebrate this feast of the 20th with distinguished companions after decorating the house with the fruits in season and inviting everyone to feast themselves'. We must, I think, put a comma before ἀξίως and take διαφ. εἰλαπιναςταῖς with ἑορτὴν ἄγειν as a dative of accompaniment or interest ('to celebrate this feast for', or 'offer a festal banquet to').

[57] Cf. Plut., *c. Epic. beatit.*, 21, p. 1102b=fr. 30 Us., Philod., π. εὐσ., p. 108 G. (Diels, *loc. cit.*, p. 893, n. 5) καὶ τῶν δογμάτων ἕκαστον πεπλασμένως, ἀλλ' οὐκ ἀπὸ ψυχῆς (Diels: τύχης N) ἐκτιθέναι, Luc., *Alex.*, 25 ἀθέων . . . ἐμπεπλῆσθαι . . . τὸν Πόντον, etc.

[58] Philod., π. εὐσ., p. 84 G. Cf. Usener, *Epicurea*, p. lxxii.

[59] Cf. *Idéal*, pp. 221ff (*Aristote dans la littérature grecque chrétienne jusqu'à Théodoret*).

[60] Against Epicurus, cf. *Life*, 3-4. Against the Christians, see almost all the Apologists. Against the pagan Mysteries, Clement of Alexandria (*Protrepticus*), Firmicus Maternus (*De err. prof. rel.*) and the Fathers *passim*.

[61] π. εὐσ., p. 104 G.=fr. 142 Us.=Diels, *Sitz. B. Berlin*, 1916, p. 894, whose readings I follow.

[62] Diels, *loc. cit.*, p. 893, n. 3 and 4, quotes fr. 839, 120 and 196 Us.; π. φύσ., κ'η', fr. 5, col. I, 5 (p. 8 Vogl.) ἀλλ[ὰ] μὰ Δία τῶμ μὲν καθ' [ἕ]κα[στ]α οὐκ ἂν φήσαιμ[εν], Epicur. pap. 1413 (unpublished), *ap.* Crönert, *Kolotes*, 104[501] ὦ πρὸς Θε[ῶν, ὅ]τι τἀτὸ ὁραῖς, Epic., π. φύσ., ι'δ', fr. 9 καὶ τῶν προσ[αγορευο]μένων φιλοσόφων οὓς ναὶ μὰ τὸ[ν Δία οἱ]μαι εἴδει (v.l. ἤδη) καὶ Δημοκριτ⟨ε⟩ίους ὀνομάσαι.

[63] As modern languages avoid the name of God (*Parbleu, morbleu, Great Scott!*), the Greek avoided that of Zeus in oaths; hence the Socratic μὰ τὸν κύνα, cf. Burnet *ad* Plato *Apol.*, 22a, 1. Epicurus here condemns this reserve (οὐ γράφων . . .), but insists that men should take seriously the calling to witness of the divinity.

[64] Philod., π. εὐσ., p. 122 G.=fr. 38 Us. I follow the text as restored by Philippson, *Hermes*, LVI, pp. 382-3: κα[λεῖ] δὲ καὶ τὸν θ[ειό]τητος [βίον ἥ]διστον καὶ μ[ακαρι]ώτατον ἐν [τῶι] περὶ ὁσιότητ[ος καὶ κ]αταξιοῖ πᾶ[ν μι]αρὸν φυλάτ[τεσθαι νοήσ]εως συ[νορω]μένης τὰ[ς τούτου] διαθέσεις [τοῦ πάν]τα γ' οἰκε[ιοῦν] τὰ γειν[ό]μεν[α] εἰς τὸν πρ[ὸς] μακ[αριότητα] τρόπον· [διὰ δὲ τοι]αῦτα νο[εῖ τε]τελέσθαι τὴν πᾶσαν ὁσιότητα σὺν τῶι τ[ὰ κοι]νὰ φυλάττειν· ὡ[ς] δ' οἱ λεγόμε-[νοι δει]σιδαίμονες εἰ[ς ἀνυ]πέρβλητον ἀ[σέβει]αν ἐκβάλλουσι[ν· οὐ]γὰρ ὁ τὴν

ἀθαν[ασίαν] κα[ὶ τ]ὴν ἄκραν μακα[ριότητ]α τοῦ θ[ε]οῦ σώ[ιζων σὺ]ν ἅπασι[ν, ἃ τ[αύταις συ]νάπτομ[εν], ἀ[[ι]]σ[εβής· εὐ]σεβὴς δ' ὁ περ[ὶ δαίμο]νος ἑκά[τε]ρον [δοξ]αζόμεν[ος]· ὁ δ' [ἐπινο]ῶν χωρὶς ὀργῆ[ς καὶ] χάριτος ἀσθενούσης τὰς ἐξ αὐτοῦ παρασκε[υὰς] τῶν ἀ[γα]θῶν κα[ὶ] τῶ[ν κακ]ῶν ἀπο[φαί]νετ' [αὐτὸν τ]ῶν ἀνθρω[πείω]ν μηδ[ε]νὸ[ς προσ]δεῖσθ', ἀλ[λὰ κατὰ σ]υντέ[λειαν εἶναι].

[65] Literally, it is our notion of God which 'understands'. Later on I regard the genitive infinitive τοῦ οἰκειοῦν as in explanatory apposition to συνορωμένης. The construction can be found in Polybius and is familiar in Biblical Greek, cf. Abel, *Gramm. du grec. bibl.*, pp. 311-12. For the idea cf. *Ep.*, III, 123 μήτε τῆς μακαριότητος ἀνοίκειον αὐτῷ προσάπτε and what follows.

[66] I think we must take ἀσθενούσης with the two nouns ὀργῆς and χάριτος.

[67] Philod., *De musica*, c. 4, 6=fr. 386, p. 258, 11 Us.

[68] Because the gods are immortal.

[69] Philod., *De dis*, I, col. VII, 1ff (p. 14 Diels).

[70] *Gn. V.*, xxxiii; fr. 602 Us.

[71] Diels, *loc. cit.*, p. 895.

[72] On this point cf. *Contemplation . . . selon Platon*, pp. 45ff (*La Contemplation religieuse*), and 358ff (*Culte public et religion du sage.*)

[73] *Contemplation*, pp. 48ff.

[74] *Tim.*, 29a 3, 6; 29e 1-30b 1.

[75] ἐτορνεύσατο 33b 6, ἀπηκριβοῦτο 33c 1.

[76] πλὴν τὸ κάλλιστον 30a 5, κάλλιον b 3, κάλλιστον . . . ἀριστόν τε ἔργον b 6, καλόν c 6, τῷ καλλίστῳ καὶ κατὰ πάντα τελέῳ d 2, καλῶς 31 b 9, δεσμῶν δὲ κάλλιστος c 2, κάλλιστα c 5, τέλεον ἐκ τελέων 32 d 1, τέλεον 33 a 7, σχῆμα τὸ πρέπον b 2, τελεώτατον b 6, κάλλιον b 8, τέλεον ἐκ τελέων 34 b 2, ὅτι λαμπρότατόν τε καὶ κάλλιστον 40 a 4 (divine stars). See also 53 e 1ff (regular polyhedra); κάλλιστα σώματα e 1, καλλίω e 5, τὰ διαφέροντα κάλλει e 7, προαιρετέον τὸ κάλλιστον 54 a 3, κάλλιον a 4, κάλλιστον a 7; 68 e 3 τὸν αὐτάρκη τε καὶ τὸν τελεώτατον θεόν (the Universe), 92 c 8, etc.

[77] Philod., *De dis*, I, col. II, 7ff (p. 10 D.).

[78] Cf. the Being of Parmenides, B 8, 32-3 οὕνεκεν οὐκ ἀτελεύτητον τὸ ἐὸν θέμις εἶναι· | ἔστι γὰρ οὐκ ἐπιδευές (*Tim.*, 33 c 4 οὐκ ἐπιδεές); Xenophanes, A 32 (pp. 122, 24, Diels-Kranz) ἐπιδεῖσθαί τε μηδενὸς αὐτῶν (τῶν θεῶν) μηδένα μηδ' ὅλως; Xenophon, *Memor.*, I, 6, 1 τὸ μηδενὸς δεῖσθαι θεῖον εἶναι; Eurip., *Herc. Fur.*, 1345 δεῖται γὰρ ὁ θεός, εἴπερ ἔστ' ὄντως θεός, | οὐδενός; Aristotle, *De Caelo*, I, 9, 279a, 34 οὔτ' ἐνδεὲς τῶν καλῶν οὐδενός ἐστιν.

[79] Tim., 33d 2 ἡγήσατο γὰρ αὐτὸ ὁ συνθεὶς αὔταρκες ὂν ἄμεινον ἔσεσθαι μᾶλλον ἢ προσδεὲς ἄλλων.

[80] τῶν ἀνθρω[πείω]ν μηδενὸ[ς προσ]δεῖσθαι, fr. 38 Us., τὸ δαιμόνιον μὲν οὐ προσδεῖταί τινος τιμῆς, fr. 386 Us., p. 258, 12.

[81] Plato, *Laws*, II, 653d-654a. Cf. *Contemplation*, pp. 53-4.

[82] Philod., *ap.* S. Ambrose, fr. 385a, p. 356, 6, Us.

[83] *Sitz. B. Berl.*, 1916, p. 895.

[84] Fr. 385 Us.

[85] Fr. 386 Us.=Philod., π. εὐσ., p. 106 G., cf. Philippson, *Hermes*, LVI, p. 373.

[86] ⟨ὁ σοφὸς προσεύχεται⟩ τοῖς θεοῖς: supplevi exempli gratia.

[87] καλεῖ τε Usener: καλείτω Diels.

[88] Fr. 386, p. 258, 15 Us.=Philod., *De dis*, III, p. 16, 14 Diels.

[89] *P. Oxyrh.*, II, 215 (p. 30)=H. Diels, *Ein Epikureisches Fragment über Götterverehrung*, *Sitz. Ber. Berlin*, 1916, pp. 886ff (text pp. 902-4). The additions inside the oblique brackets are due to Diels, in his German translation facing the

text. These additions are, of course, only intended to indicate the sequence of thought and make no claim to certainty.

[90] [κ]αὶ τού[τοις] βο[ύ]λομαι πάντα κα[τ]αθύειν καὶ τούτοις [ἀν]ατίθεναι, ll. 8-11. πάντα, I think, belongs to both verbs.

[91] ἄλλων ἰδιω[τῶ]ν, l, 13. 'Als andere Laien' (Diels), i.e. 'laymen' as opposed to the φιλόσοφος is clearly possible but seems to me a little far-fetched.

## CHAPTER V

### EPICURUS AND THE ASTRAL RELIGION

GODS who would do no evil; gods who would not be malicious; gods who would not be all the time watching your smallest actions to see whether you overstepped the bounds, the narrow bounds imposed on man, nor looking out for your slightest slip so as to strike you down, all the time knowing well that one day you would fall into their hands and they could satisfy their thirst for revenge. Gods, in short, without hate and without envy. That is the good news that Epicurus gave to the world, with an insistence in which we may perhaps discern the memory of a personal and painful struggle from which he had slowly freed himself and from which he afterwards burned to free others.

Was it to be expected that after that he would accept the new religion propounded by the learned, his rivals in the school of Plato and Aristotle?[1] I have already described the origin and *raison d'être* of this astral religion. The problem before the educated was to find an object of worship which would satisfy at once the demands of scientific thought and the needs of the religious soul. The gods of the vulgar offended against morality and had no connection with the order of the Cosmos. As early as the *Republic*[2] Plato had banished those lying fables which pictured the gods as being as much a prey to passion and as capable of crime as men. In the *Timaeus* (40 d 6ff), it is with well-marked irony that he leaves the task of speaking about the genealogies of the traditional gods to the 'sons of gods', that is, to the authors of theogonies who, like the Orphics, were considered to be descended from the gods.[3] As regards the traditional gods, who could not be seen,[4] it was possible to indulge in all kinds of fancy, because the hearer was incapable of verifying what was said to him.[5] This is equivalent to saying that the popular gods escaped from the grip of science. Now in certain circles at least it was no longer possible to accept a theory which was not scientific, even a theory about the gods. The Divinity had to be not only the guarantee of morality, but the support of the cosmic order, the supreme law of the Universe. That is very much the rôle which the science of astronomy, which had made such great strides in the fourth century, assigned to the Heavens and the stars. The movement of the Heavens controls all other movements. The orbits of the stars had been reduced to regular periods which were obedient to number and which measured time. All that area of the Cosmos beyond the moon formed thus a harmonious unity, of everlasting duration.[6] Besides, the Heavens and stars were gods indeed. Their unending movement was an ordered movement, which implied that they were endowed with an intelligent soul. They were, then, living, immortal beings. Had that not been from all antiquity the definition of gods?[7]

But then in Epicurus' eyes no advance had been made at all, and this religion of the learned was no better than the other, being designed to inspire the same fear as the popular religion. Just as the old gods had been, so these new gods were endowed with a will of their own whose inflexible decrees laid on humanity a yoke more unbearable then the caprices of the Olympians. According to Plato in the *Timaeus* (47 c 3) the regular movements of the Divine Heavens admit of absolutely no error.[8] In the *Laws* (vii, 818 b ff), this perfectly unchangeable character of the celestial movements is called 'a necessity, against which even God cannot strive'[9] and is defined in these terms (vii, 818 b 9): 'This divine necessity' — as opposed to human necessities (818 b 4) — 'is, I presume, that without practising which, or without having studied it, no God at all, nor Genius, nor Hero[10] would be capable of seriously exercising providential care over mankind.' Finally the *Epinomis* asserts (982 b 5 -c 5): 'The necessity inhering in a soul endowed with intelligence is without doubt by far the strongest of all necessities — for it legislates as master, being ruled by no one — and this immutable decree, once the soul has decided on the best in accordance with the best purpose, is that which is fulfilled in fact, according to the plan; there is no metal so hard[11] that it could be more resistant or more unalterable, but in very truth the three Fates that guard it watch over the fulfilment of the decree approved in accordance with the most just deliberation by each one of the gods of the stars.' In the same way for Aristotle the movement of the stars was voluntary,[12] and this unchangeable movement necessarily conferred on them the rank of first and sovereign beings in the Universe.[13] Finally, if it is added that by their conjunctions and oppositions, which make them appear, vanish, and then appear again to our eyes, these star-gods 'frighten men unable to calculate,[14] who think that they see in the sky signs which foretell the future',[15] we shall easily understand why Epicurus regarded the astral religion as even more dangerous than the beliefs of the people.

What, in fact, did the new prophets teach? On the one hand, that the order instituted by the stars was absolutely inflexible; on the other, that the stars were animate beings, endowed with sense and reason, and therefore personal gods. The result of the conjunction of these two features is apparent at once.

It had been a very old-established belief that everything in this world was dependent on the gods. But the gods being thought of as personal beings, liable to human passions and therefore to feelings of mercy and pity, it was possible to hope to sway them by means of prayer and sacrifice. In this way fear did not entirely dominate the heart of man; hope was there too. However hard one's present lot might appear it was allowable to expect a change for the better. And this same hope remained at hand afterwards, when, to the universally prevalent belief in the omnipotence of Fate there had been joined the faith in saviour gods more powerful than Heimarmene.[16] For if men could not expect to have any power over the irresistible march of happenings fixed from all eternity by the regular interaction of the celestial movements, and if it was in vain for them to be incensed by the fact, they could at least influence the personal gods who would save them from Heimarmene. But what could be done if the only real gods were at the same time the gods who fixed unalterably the course of events? What means was there of appeasing or moving them if thenceforward they were one with the order of necessity? And what help was there against them once there were no other gods and they alone possessed those attributes of animation, sensibility, and free will which men had always been accustomed to apply to the idea of divinity?

Henceforward there was no room for anything but fear and boundless despair. It would have been better, indeed, to have banished utterly the belief in gods. There would then have been nothing but blind Fate, the 'Law of Nature', an entirely material law that no one would have thought of rebelling against any more than we rebel against the stone which trips us or the wind which burns or freezes us. But what were men to think of the immutable decrees which proceeded from free wills? How could they help thinking that such decrees revealed a constant will to do harm to mankind, that the whole preoccupation of the gods was to make them suffer, and suffer without any remission for the rest of infinite time? For it was not even possible for them to tell each other that everything ended at death. The learned would not have it. The human soul, everlasting as the stars, was subject to the laws of destiny.[17] Attached at first to a fixed star,[18] it came down from this star by virtue of necessity (ἐξ ἀνάγκης 42 a 3) for its first birth in a human body. Its future lot depended on the manner in which it had lived this first life. If it had lived well it went up again to a σύννομον ἄστρον where it passed a life of happiness similar to the life of the star. If it had lived badly it was born anew, and entered on an indefinite number of existences, passing first into the body of a woman and then into the bodies of animals. And if the soul persisted in its evil ways it would never see the end of its tribulations and sufferings until it had brought into subjection to the regular movements of the intellect all the passions which had been joined to its being from the material body (*Tim.*, 42 c-d). That, then, was what awaited the soul according to the moral and religious teaching of Plato and the Academy. From which it followed that far from avoiding the faults of the traditional morality and religion, these new dogmas, in the eyes of Epicurus, could only make them worse; Hell was henceforward this earthly life itself, or rather an indefinite succession of earthly lives, of which each one would surpass in horror those that went before it because the soul was incarnated in beasts which became ever more vicious.

What, then, was the good of banishing the fears and hopes aroused by the traditional gods if the cult of the divine stars had to be adopted? But it was easy to overthrow the whole edifice from its foundations. The astral religion was protected by the magical name of science; it was, then, sufficient to show that this science was false, that these supposed divine stars had nothing of the divine in them because they were only an agglomerated mass of fire. This is the task Epicurus sets himself in the letter to Herodotus, and he himself again or his compiler in the letter to Pythocles; it is worth while reproducing these texts, for they take on a new interest if we put them back into the spiritual atmosphere of the age.

*The Letter to Pythocles*, 76–82:

'We must not believe that the motions and turnings[19] of the heavenly bodies, their eclipses, their risings and settings and all the phenomena of this kind, are produced under the influence of a Being who has their direction assigned to him as a public duty (λειτουργοῦντος), who controls or always will control these phenomena at the same time as he enjoys perfect bliss together with immortality – [77] for troubles, anxieties and the emotions of anger and benevolence are not consistent with happiness but arise where there is weakness and fear and the need of help from others – nor must we believe that the stars, which are nothing but agglomerated fire, are in possession of blessedness and, taking charge of these movements, control them as they wish.[20] But we must preserve in full the majesty of the divine in all the expressions which we apply to such ideas,[21] so that there may not arise from them any opinions contradictory to the majesty of the divine. Otherwise the contradiction will of itself produce the greatest disturbance in men's souls. Therefore, we must think that this 'necessity' and this 'regular revolution' of the stars[22] results from the formation, at the time when the world came into being, of those aforesaid agglomerations in which matter was caught up.

[78] Furthermore, we must think that the special function of the study of nature is to discover exactly the cause of the essential realities (τὰ κυριώτατα), and that happiness in the knowledge of celestial phenomena lies precisely in this exact discovery, and in the understanding of the kinds of beings which are seen in these celestial phenomena and of everything which is akin to that exact science which is necessary for happiness. We must think, also, that there is no place here for anything which admits of several explanations or can occur in different ways, and that, in short, there is no place in what is immortal and blessed for any of the things which are open to dispute or hint at disturbance. And we can apprehend by thought that this is absolutely so.

'[79] As to that which falls within the domain of the detailed investigation of settings, rising, turnings, eclipses and everything of that kind, all this contributes nothing to the happiness which knowledge brings; far from it, those who have observed these phenomena but still do not know what are their natures and their essential causes are subject to the same terrors as if they had not acquired this excess of knowledge (προσῄδεισαν),[23] and perhaps to even greater terrors, since the reverential awe (θάμβος) which this excess of observations (προσκατανοήσεως) arouses in them cannot discover the solution or understand the regulation of essential realities. Therefore, even if we discover a plurality of causes for the turnings, settings, risings, eclipses and everything of that kind, as was the case already when we were dealing with specific phenomena ⟨in this world⟩, [80] we should not believe that our enquiries into these subjects have not reached the required degree of exactness to contribute to our peace of mind and our happiness. And so, considering in comparison with ⟨celestial phenomena⟩ (παραθεωροῦντας), in how many ways a similar phenomenon arises on earth, we must reason similarly about the causes of celestial phenomena and about all that is not evident to the senses,[24] despising those who cannot distinguish, in the case of things whose appearance is only visible to us from a long way off,[25] either that which exists or is produced in one way only, or that which can happen in more than one way, and who also do not know in what conditions it is impossible to preserve the peace of the soul and in what conditions it is still possible to do so.[26] If then we think that a phenomenon can be produced in some other way also, because we observe accurately that it can arise in more than one way, we shall not be any more concerned than if we know it arises in some particular way.

'[81] Besides all these general remarks we must grasp this point, that the principal disturbance for the minds of men arises because they regard the celestial bodies as blessed and immortal at the same time as they attribute to them wills, actions, and motives in contradiction with those two characteristics, and because, on the authority of myths, they are always expecting or wondering about some terrible and eternal punishment or even because they dread the lack of feeling which is proper to the state of death, as though it must affect us in some way,[27] and because, lastly, they submit to these fears not as a result of mature opinion but of some irrational suggestion, so that, as they do not define the danger which is to come, they suffer a disturbance as severe or even more extensive than if they had formed an opinion on these matters. [82] Peace of mind consists in being delivered from all these fears and in keeping constantly in mind the general and essential truths.

'Consequently we must pay attention to the immediate data of our internal feelings and external sensations, following common judgment when we have to deal with common sensations and our own when we have to deal with personal sensations, judging every intuition of the moment in accordance with each of these criteria. For if we give our attention to these data we shall thoroughly uncover the true cause whence arose our worry and fear and, perceiving the cause of celestial phenomena and of all the other happenings as they occur (τῶν ἀεὶ παρεμπιπτόντων), we shall free ourselves from everything which arouses the worst terrors in other men.'

*The Letter to Pythocles*, 85, 9–88, 3

'Firstly, then, we must be satisfied that there is no other object to be gained from the knowledge of celestial phenomena, whether we consider them in connexion with other studies or separately, but peace of mind and a resolute confidence, just as with the other branches of research. [86] We must not force the facts to fit an impossible explanation nor adopt a method of research similar in all ways to that which we employ when we are considering modes of life or the solution of other problems of physics, as for example that "the Universe is composed of body and the intangible essence (i.e. void)", or that "the elements are indivisible", and all other such propositions which only admit of one explanation in harmony with the evidence of the senses. This is not so with the celestial phenomena; these latter can arise through more than one cause and their essence can be defined by many predications all of which are equally in harmony with our sensations. For we must not conduct the study of nature in accordance with empty assumptions and arbitrary rules but in agreement with the demands of the phenomena; [87] what our life needs is not subjective theories[28] nor superficial opinions but the means of living without disturbance.

'Now everything goes on unshaken as regards all those things which admit of many solutions in harmony with the phenomena once we admit, as we should, a probable explanation of them; but if we accept one theory and reject another which would fit the phenomena equally well, it is clear that we are completely abandoning the sphere of scientific study and drifting into mythology. Now we must apply to what is performed in the sky certain indications given us by phenomena on earth for we can observe how they arise while we cannot do so in the case of the celestial phenomena; the latter indeed admit of more than one explanation of their coming into existence. [88] Nevertheless we must always pay attention to the appearance of each of these phenomena and as to opinions which are grafted on to that appearance we must distinguish the phenomena about whose production it is possible to advance various explanations without conflicting with the evidence of phenomena on earth.'

From the rest of the letter I will select a number of aphorisms which support one or other of the theses set out so far.

*On agreement with the evidence of the senses* (φαινόμενα); 90, 4. None of the worlds which are formed in the void can grow to the point where it collides with another world 'as some of the so-called *physikoi* say (i.e. Democritus); for this doctrine is in contradiction with the phenomena'.

91, 6. The size of the sun, the moon and the stars is, relatively to us, exactly as it appears to us. 'Every objection on this point will be easily removed if we pay attention to the self-evident testimony of the senses, as I show in my *Books on Nature*.'[29]

*On the possibility of giving, for the same fact, several explanations all equally agreeing with the evidence of the senses.*

93, 8. 'For none of these explanations (of the solstices) or of those which could be advanced in a similar vein is at variance with any of the convincing evidence of the senses, provided that, in such branches of enquiry, we constantly pay attention to the possible and can refer each point to what is in harmony with the phenomena without fearing the servile artifices of the astronomers.'

94, 1. The waxing and waning of the moon can be due to more than one cause. 'We can have recourse to all the kinds of explanation suggested to us by the phenomena of this world to account for these aspects of the moon on condition that we do not, infatuated with the method of the single explanation, reject groundlessly the other methods simply because we have not considered what it is possible for men to observe and what impossible, and as a result yearn to observe the impossible. Besides, the moon may shine with her own light or she may shine with the sun's. In fact we see many things on earth also shining with their own light and many others taking their light from elsewhere. None of the celestial phenomena is at variance with these explanations if we remember the method of multiple explanation, if we consider in a single survey the whole collection of hypotheses and explanations in harmony with the phenomena, and if we do not cast our eyes on inharmonious explanations and puff them up with artificial importance, or relapse, in one way or another, into the method of the single explanation. The impression we receive of a face in the moon can be due to variations of the parts of the moon's surface, or to the interposing of other bodies, or to any other of the numerous explanations which might be considered, provided that they are in harmony with the phenomena. In anything to do with celestial phenomena we must never cease to follow in this track; for if a man enters into a struggle with the self-evident testimony of the senses he will never be able to share in true peace of mind.'[30]

*That we should not attribute the order of the Heavens to a divine government.*

97, 1. 'The regular order of the revolutions of the celestial bodies must be regarded in the same way as some of the happenings on earth. And let us not at any price introduce the divine nature into this matter; that must be kept free of all public service (ἀλειτούργητος), in the fullness of its happiness. If we do otherwise all enquiry into the causes of celestial phenomena will be nothing but empty talk, as it has already become for some who have not held firm to the way of the possible but have fallen into the futility of believing that things cannot happen except in one way and of rejecting all the other ways in harmony with the possible, because, being carried away towards inconceivable ideas, in their contemplation of the sky they lose sight of the earthly phenomena which should provide us with indications.'

113, 8. 'To give a single cause for these phenomena (the movements of the stars, regular or irregular) when they invite a plurality of explanations is sheer madness. This unseemly practice belongs to people attached to the vain methods of astronomy who assign futile causes to certain phenomena while they in no way free the divine nature from the burden of public service (λειτουργιῶν).'

115, 9. 'The signs of the weather which are seen in certain animals are due to a chance conjuncture of circumstances.[31] For these signs do not bring any necessity to compel bad weather to follow inevitably, nor is there a divine nature which sits to watch the outgoings of these animals and then brings to pass[32] the happenings foretold by these signs. Any living thing, no matter how small the understanding it had, would guard against falling into such folly, and all the more would the being who possesses the fullness of happiness.'

*That myths must be banished.*

104, 1-4. 'There are still many more possible explanations of the production of the thunderbolt; it is enough that myth is excluded, as it will be if we follow the indications given by things which are obvious and reason correctly by inference about those which are not obvious.'[33]

Finally, we may add to this account of the two letters nos. x–xiii of the *Principal Doctrines* which form a single group. *k.d.*, x. 'If the means by which the debauched seek pleasure could free their souls from fear about the celestial phenomena as well as from the fear of death and pains, and if it taught them the limited nature of desires and pains we should never have anything to reproach them with. . . .'

xi. 'If we were not in any way worried by our suspicions about celestial phenomena and death, fearing lest these things are important for us, and also by our inability to understand that sufferings and desires have a limited character, we should have no need of the study of nature.'

xii. 'It is impossible to banish fear about the most essential matters if we do not know what is the nature of the Universe but suspect that there may be some truth in what the myths say. So that without the study of nature it is impossible for the pleasures we taste to be entirely unalloyed.'

xiii. 'There is no profit in making oneself secure from men while suspicions remain about the things above, or the things beneath the earth, or in general about the things in unlimited space.'[34]

If we wished to define in a word the moral attitude which the Sages of Greece were most ready to extol towards the end of the fourth century we should perhaps choose the word *ataraxia*.

All the beliefs most deeply rooted in the Greek mind had been radically upset. For the free citizens of the little Hellenic cities, jealous of their autonomy and their privileges, nothing was more abiding than the horror of tyranny; but now they obeyed tyrants and little by little, as a result of the slow moral dissolution which tyranny engenders, they were becoming accustomed to this obedience; worse still, the tyrant was flattered, deified, and on the way to being regarded as the only god. For the artisan at Athens, who had been taught to read with the poems of Homer, who had attended the dramatic performances in the theatre of Dionysus, and who had heard the orators of the people in the Assembly, nothing was more assured than the conviction that Greek was superior to barbarian; but now Greeks and barbarians formed one and the same people, breathing the same air, enjoying the same sun, forming a part of one great family which included all men.[35] It had been a settled belief of the Greek mind that power and glory joined to a long life were the conditions of happiness. Now Alexander had undoubtedly conquered the world, no glory equalled his; but he was dead at thirty-three (356-323). What then could be more fruitless than his prodigious exploits? And since the death of Alexander his generals had not ceased to struggle for the Empire. They all had only one cry on their lips, 'to free Greece', but in fact they were moved only by the same crude appetite for domination, quarrelling among themselves like children.

When a man reflected on the fate of the human race how could he avoid wishing to lead a hidden life? How could he avoid aspiring to peace of soul? That was the key to happiness and the last word in wisdom.

Epicurus (341-270) taught that we must make ourselves secure against men and gods, against our own desires and fears, and so, armed against every attack, work with a few friends to preserve serenity of soul which he compares to the calm expanse of the sea when no breeze ruffles it (πρὸς γαληνισμόν, *Ep.* I, 83,13).

Pyrrho of Elis (c. 365-275), without writing anything, gave in his life the perfect example of a man entirely dead to all desire. Some have been astonished at such indifference and, considering it un-Greek, have concluded that Pyrrho must have come under the influence of the Indian gymnosophists.[36] This is possible, but it seems to me that starting from the same experience, the agonies and doubts of the age, and one common philosophic idea, the εὐθυμίη of Democritus, a perfectly logical progression led Epicurus and Pyrrho to the same conclusion, the extinction of desire, with the difference, however, that Pyrrho carried his universal detachment further. Be that as it may, the end sought is identical. If the word ἀταραξία is the *leitmotiv* of Epicurus, it defines no less accurately the attitude of Pyrrho. 'Pyrrho of Elis has left no writings but his disciple Timon says that he who would be happy must consider these three points; first, what things are in themselves, second, what disposition we must adopt towards them, and last, what is the result for us of this disposition. Now,

'(*a*) Things are all indifferent, equally uncertain and indeterminate. . . .

'(*b*) Whatever we are speaking about we shall say that we must not affirm it more than we deny it; or that we must affirm and deny it at one and the same time; or that we must neither affirm nor deny it.

'(*c*) If we adopt this disposition, says Timon, we shall attain first *aphasia*, and then *ataraxia*.'[37] This point of doctrine is firmly established. Diogenes Laertius repeats it in the same terms: 'The end according to the Sceptics is the suspension of judgment (ἐποχή) which *ataraxia* follows like a shadow, as we are told by Timon and Aenesidemus',[38] and similarly Sextus Empiricus: 'The Sceptics hoped to attain *ataraxia* by the examination of the uncertainty belonging to the evidence of the senses and to our concepts; and when this examination proved impossible for them they suspended judgment (ἐπέσχον). Now as they acted thus, as by chance (οἷον τυχικῶς), *ataraxia* followed this suspension of judgment as the shadow follows the substance.'[39]

Furthermore, the resemblances between Pyrrho and Epicurus do not end there. Epicurus was seen to be always patient and gentle in the midst of evils without number and people could not help attributing so remarkable a steadfastness to some divine quality. The feeling is similar to that inspired by the spectacle of the 'indifference', the 'apathy', shown by the Sage of Elis. Timon wondered at the way he remained 'in deep tranquillity of spirit, always free from care, always self-possessed and unmoved by anything, indifferent to the specious fables of science'.[40] Elsewhere, to depict the Sage's peace of mind, Timon turns to the Epicurean image of the dead calm of the sea (γαλήνη).[41] And just as Colotes called his master a god, and others compared Epicurus to the sun which drives the darkness away, so Timon also cannot help comparing the radiant influence of Pyrrho to that of the sun god: 'This, Pyrrho, is what I would know. How, when you are only a man, do you live a life so easy and so peaceable? How can you guide men, like to the god who drives all round the earth and discloses to our eyes the flaming orb of his sphere?'[42] Is this merely gross flattery? I do not think so. He who in times of misery[43] gave an example and revealed the secret of a wonderfully balanced[44] way of life must have appeared to a young disciple as a being comparable to a god.

Indifference, *apathy*, *ataraxia*: this attitude, common, in varying degrees, to Pyrrho and Epicurus, we meet again lastly in the school of the Porch, founded by Zeno in Athens in 301. Once again, the object is to make oneself indifferent to everything which is not the true good,[45] insensible to the blows of Fortune,[46] and proof against the unsettling influences of desire and fear.[47] Nevertheless, there remains a vital difference between the *ataraxia* of Pyrrho or Epicurus and that of Zeno.

Pyrrhonian detachment had no dealings whatever with the science of celestial bodies in favour in the Academy, nor with the new religion which had sprung from it. If things 'are all indifferent, equally uncertain and indeterminate', it is much better to suspend judgment. But, on the other hand, we must live; and since we have only one life we must try to live it as happily as possible. Scepticism is out of place in questions of human conduct. Pyrrho, here dogmatic,[48] taught that happiness lies in total indifference; that is the divine, the sovereign good from which flows a perfectly balanced life.[49] There is then no question of bringing one's soul into agreement with the harmony of the Whole. Do we know what this Whole is, or whether a universal Order exists? Such enquiries cannot but unsettle the soul. Happy is the man who, like Pyrrho, has been able to free himself from the specious fables of science.[50]

As to the Epicurean doctrine of *ataraxia*, far from being in any way dependent on the science of the Heavens and the religion of the divine stars, it engaged in open warfare with these new Platonic dogmas. For if we make the celestial movements into the image of Necessity itself, and attribute this Necessity to divine wills, the result is that all happenings on earth will be ordained by decree of the gods. And as these happenings are most often distressing we shall have to think that the gods pursue us with their hatred, a hatred which cannot be turned aside and will never cease. This is to make the reign of fear everlasting; there is no error more pernicious.

Stoicism, by contrast, was based on a cosmology closely connected with that of the Academy. It admitted the necessary character of the celestial movements, it saw in these movements the manifestation of a divine Reason, and it asserted that this Reason controlled all earthly happenings by an inflexible law. Yet at the same time it proclaimed the ethical teaching of *ataraxia*, it taught that the Sage was never disturbed and never swayed by fear. More than that, this doctrine of *ataraxia* was not, in Stoicism, an added element, unconnected with the science of the world. The Sage did not seek to ignore the world order or to escape from the meshes of Destiny, far from it, it was precisely because he understood this order and submitted to it that he enjoyed an immutable peace.

Towards the end of a life which had been fraught with ordeals the aged Plato, in the *Timaeus* (90 d-e), laid it down that peace of soul is achieved by the knowledge of the harmony and the revolutions of the Whole. 'He who contemplates,' he said, 'must make himself like the object of his contemplation, in accordance with the original nature.[51] Then, when this likeness has been achieved, the wise man will reach the goal of the perfect life which the gods have ordained for men, both in the present and for the future.' Some years later, in his last work (*Laws*, X 903 b-d) Plato showed how imprudent it is, as well as useless, to be angry with one's lot. 'For He who takes care of the Whole has ordained all things with a view to the safety and well-being of the Whole so that for each part, in proportion to its powers, the evils it suffers and the actions it originates are exactly those which are suitable for it.'

That is the soil in which the moral doctrine of the Porch was rooted. One could adopt complete indifference towards the science of Plato, as Pyrrho did, and base a theory of happiness on a kind of technique of renunciation. Or one could meet science with science, as Epicurus did, drive every divine principle out of the Universe and in a world thus emptied of God seek the means of living happily by the sole method of limiting one's desires. Finally, one could accept the constraints of a universal Reason and regard it as wise and good, recognize a Providence in this Necessity and so bring one's will into agreement with the Will that moves the Whole. One could sing with Cleanthes:

> Guide me, O Zeus, and thou, my Destiny,
> Towards the place your decrees assign to me.
> I will obey without murmuring.[52]

That too was a way towards tranquillity of soul. It was the way taken by the Stoics with a conviction so strong and fervent that it won a multitude of adherents, inspired some of the finest acts of heroism in the Ancient World and, at long intervals, made wisdom reign among the governors of the Hellenistic monarchies and the Empire.[53]

But this wisdom was a religion. By its doctrine of a God who was present everywhere and active everywhere it sanctioned, indeed it counselled, conferences with the Divinity. Marcus Aurelius was a kind of mystic, and Epictetus has left us prayers whose tone is admirable. And this Stoic religion was essentially a cosmic religion. The hymn of Cleanthes is in honour of the Soul of the world or the God of the world:

> All the Universe that wheels about the earth,
> 'Tis thee it obeys; it goes where thou dost lead it.[54]

It was by fixing his eyes always on the Universal Order[55] that Marcus Aurelius strengthened himself in his solitude, 'You must one day realize at last of what universe you are a part and from what Governor of the universe your existence comes, and that a limit of time has been set aside for you, and if you do not use it to clear away the clouds from your mind (εἰς τὸ ἀπαιθριάσαι), it will be gone, and you will be gone, and it will never return again' (II, 4).

So man, weak, fallible, and the creature of a day, turned for his support to the omnipotence, the omniscience, and the eternity of God. Hence arose a mysticism which, kindling its earliest flame in the *Timaeus*, shone with its greatest brilliance among the disciples of Zeno.

## NOTES

[1] On the long-lasting quarrel between Epicurus and the 'Platonic-Peripatetic' school, cf. especially the work, already cited, by Bignone, *L'Aristotele perduto* etc. On the divine stars, *ib.*, II, pp. 355-538.

[2] II, 377e-391e Cf. *Id. rel. d. Grecs*, pp. 176 and n. 3, 192-5.

[3] *Rep.*, II, 364e 3 βίβλων δὲ ὅμαδον παρέχονται Μουσαίου καὶ 'Ορφέως Σελήνης τε καὶ Μουσῶν ἐκγόνων, ὥς φασι.

[4] As opposed to the divine stars which are visible: *Tim.*, 40d 5 θεῶν ὁρατῶν, 41a 4 ὅσοι δὲ περιπολοῦσιν φανερῶς καὶ ὅσοι καθ'ὅσον ἂν ἐθέλωσιν, *Epin.*, 984d 3ff: the opposition of the traditional gods (Zeus, Hera, and 'all the others') to gods ὁρατοί, μέγιστοι καὶ τιμιώτατοι.

[5] *Critias*, 107b 1 ἡ γὰρ ἀπειρία καὶ σφόδρα ἄγνοια τῶν ἀκουόντων περὶ ὧν ἂν οὕτως ἔχωσιν πολλὴν εὐπορίαν παρέχεσθον τῷ μέλλοντι λέγειν τι περὶ αὐτῶν. Cp. Hippocr., π. ἀρχ. ἰητρ., 1, p. 36, 18 Heib. οἷον περὶ τῶν μετεώρων ἢ τῶν ὑπὸ γῆν· ἃ εἴ τις λέγοι καὶ γινώσκοι ὡς ἔχει, οὔτ' ἂν αὐτῷ τῷ λέγοντι οὔτε τοῖς ἀκούουσιν δῆλα ἂν εἴη, εἴτε ἀληθέα ἐστιν εἴτε μή· οὐ γὰρ ἔστι, πρὸς ὅ τι χρὴ ἀνέγκαντα εἰδέναι τὸ σαφές.

[6] Cf. Arist., *De Caelo*, I, 10-12 and II, 1.

[7] *Ib.*, II, 1, 284a 2 διόπερ καλῶς ἔχει συμπείθειν ἑαυτὸν τοὺς ἀρχαίους καὶ μάλιστα πατρίους ἡμῶν ἀληθεῖς εἶναι λόγους, ὡς ἔστιν ἀθάνατόν τι καὶ θεῖον τῶν ἐχόντων μὲν κίνησιν κτλ., 284a, 11 τὸν δ' οὐρανὸν καὶ τὸν ἄνω τόπον οἱ μὲν ἀρχαῖοι τοῖς θεοῖς ἀπένειμαν ὡς ὄντα μόνον ἀθάνατον.

[8] μιμούμενοι τὰς τοῦ θεοῦ (sc. περιόδους) πάντως ἀπλανεῖς οὔσας, Tim., 47e 3.

[9] *Laws*, VII, 818b 2, cf. V, 741a, and *Protag.*, 345b.

[10] Heroes exercised a protecting and benevolent influence over the cities which guarded their relics.

[11] οὐδὲ ἀδάμας. We hardly know what metal the Ancients understood by ἀδάμας, cf. *Tim.*, 59b 5 and Taylor, *ad loc.* The meaning 'diamond' does not occur before Theophrastus, *Lap.*, 19.

[12] Fr. 24 R. = Cic., *N.D.*, II, 16 *restat ut motus astrorum sit voluntarius.*

[13] Fr. 6 R. = Simpl., *In de cael.* (I, 9, 279a 18), p. 288, 30 Heib. τὸ θεῖον ἀμετάβλητον ἀναγκαῖον εἶναι πᾶν τὸ πρῶτον καὶ ἀκρότατον.

[14] τοῖς οὐ δυναμένοις λογίζεσθαι, *Tim.*, 40d 2. Those who can calculate, that is the astronomers, know that the conjunctions of the stars take place at the proper time as a result of the various movements of the various stars; these phenomena, therefore, do not surprise them and they see no predictions in them, cf. Taylor,

*ad loc.* It is interesting to note that, though Cicero still read οὐ before δυναμένοις (*rationis expertibus*), this οὐ had disappeared by the time of Chalcidius (*iis qui motus earum intelligere possunt*) and of Proclus (III, 145, 8; 150, 30 D.), and that of all the manuscripts, A (codex of Arethas, 9th century) is the only one to have it: even there οὐ is dotted by A². As Taylor notes, p. 244, the rapid spread of astrology after Cicero's time caused this οὐ to be considered an error: it is indeed 'those who calculate', the astrologers, who predict the future from the stars.

[15] Tim., 40d 1-2. This passage might refer simply to the eclipses of the sun and moon by which the Greek was not less terrified than the other peoples of antiquity (cf. Thuc., VII, 50). But the complexity of the phenomena mentioned in the text makes us think rather, even at this date, of the divinatory operations of astrology. In that case Plato must be alluding to oriental peoples, for astrology properly so-called had not yet penetrated into Greece even in his day, cf. Taylor, *ad loc.*, who quotes Proclus, *in Tim.*, III, 151, 1ff: 'It is with considerable astonishment that Theophrastus contemplates the science of the Chaldaeans of his time concerning the celestial phenomena, a science which predicted among other things the life and death of each individual, and not only general happenings, as for example good and bad weather (thus attributing to the Chaldaeans the doctrine that the planet Hermes appearing in winter causes severe cold and in summer burning heat). The Chaldaeans in fact, says Theophrastus in his book *On Predictions*, knew in advance according to the state of the heavens both particular and general happenings.'

[16] Cf. *Id. rel. d. Gr.*, pp. 101ff ('Ειμαρμένη).

[17] νόμους τε τοὺς εἱμαρμένους, *Tim.*, 41e 2. In spite of the excellent article of Gundel, *P.W.*, VII, 2622ff, there is still something to be said about the evolution of the term and the idea. Here I will restrict myself to mentioning two points.

(a) It does not seem to me that ἡ εἱμαρμένη (sc. μοῖρα) had been used as a noun before Plato. The idea comes perhaps from the Ionian philosophers (so Gundel), but on this point we only have much later δόξαι (written at a time when the term and the idea were common); there is no text even from the Pre-Socratics (cf. Diels-Kranz, s.v. εἱμαρμένος and Diels's note to [Heracleitus], B 137, I, p. 182, 4 n.cr.). On the other hand the tragic poets have εἵμαρται and εἱμαρμένον ἐστι, not the participle used as a noun.

(b) Whereas εἵμαρται is as a rule still linked to the idea of divinity before Plato – cf. besides the μοῖρα θεῶν of Homer (v. gr. Od., III, 269), Theognis, 1033-4 θεῶν δ' εἱμαρμένα δῶρα | οὐκ ἂν ῥηϊδίως θνητὸς ἀνὴρ προφύγοι, Aeschylus, *Agam.*, 913-14 τὰ δ'ἄλλα φρόντις . . . | θήσει δικαίως σὺν θεοῖς εἱμαρμένα, Sophocles, *Trach.*, 169 πρὸς θεῶν εἱμαρμένα, Bacchylides, 13, 1 (Jebb=41, 1 Edmonds) εὖ μὲν εἱμάρθαι παρὰ δαίμονος ἀν|θρώποις ἄριστον, – in Plato εἱμαρμένη appears alone; *Phaedo*, 115a 5 ἐμὲ δὲ νῦν ἤδη καλεῖ, φαίη ἂν ἀνὴρ τραγικός, ἡ εἱμαρμένη, *Timaeus*, 89c, 6 παρὰ τὴν εἱμαρμένην (μοῖραν) τοῦ χρόνου (this indeed equivalent to the χρόνος εἱμαρμένος of Phaedo, 113a 2-3 οὗ [the marsh of Acheron] αἱ τῶν τετελευτηκότων ψυχαὶ τῶν πολλῶν ἀφικνοῦνται καί τινας εἱμαρμένους χρόνους μείνασαι . . . πάλιν ἐκπέμπονται εἰς τὰς τῶν ζῴων γενέσεις).

[18] Tim., 41e 1; cf. Taylor, *ad loc.*

[19] τροπή in the singular. The reference, then, is not only to the turning of the sun at the two tropics, north and south – τροπαί = solstices – but to every turning of the heavenly bodies.

[20] κατὰ βούλησιν, 77, 5. Cf. 81, 4 ἔχειν βουλήσεις ἅμα καὶ πράξεις. An answer to the *motus voluntarius* of the stars according to Plato and Aristotle (Arist., fr. 24 R.).

[21] κατὰ πάντα ὀνόματα φερόμενα ἐπὶ τῆς τοιαύτης ἐννοίας. In everything that we

think and say about the stars we must be careful of the majesty of the godhead and not degrade it by regarding stars as gods.

[22] Another certain allusion to the Platonists. For ἀνάγκη cf. Laws, VII, 818a 8 τὸ δὲ ἀναγκαῖον αὐτῶν (of numbers and the stars), 818b 2 οὐδὲ θεὸς ἀνάγκῃ μή ποτε φανῇ μαχόμενος, 818b 3 ὅσαι θεῖαί γε, οἶμαι, τῶν ἀναγκῶν εἰσίν and the following sections 818b-c, *Epin.*, 982b, 5 ἡ ψυχῆς δὲ ἀνάγκη νοῦν κεκτημένης ἁπασῶν ἀναγκῶν πολὺ μεγίστη γίγνοιτ' ἄν, κτλ. For περίοδος, cf. *Tim.*, 34a, 1ff. κίνησιν γὰρ ἀπένειμεν αὐτῷ (the Heavens) τὴν . . . περὶ νοῦν καὶ φρόνησιν μάλιστα οὖσαν· . . . ἐπὶ δὲ τὴν περίοδον ταύτην, 43c 7 the regular περίοδοι of the soul (connected with those of the stars) are opposed to the fortuitous and irregular movements which affect small children by reason of the violence of their sense impressions. περίοδος implies in itself the idea of a regular movement.

[23] There is no reason to correct to προσῄδεσαν (von der Muehll). The orthography ᾔδεισαν will be found in the Septuagint and Strabo; this is one of the anomalies of which Epicurus offers more than one example and which Bignone explains by his long stay in Ionia. As to the meaning, this Epicurean use of πρόσοιδα should be added in Liddell-Scott-Jones, *s.v.*

[24] ὑπέρ τε τῶν μετεώρων καὶ παντὸς τοῦ ἀδήλου 80, 4-5. Cf. Hippocr., π. ἀρχ. ἰητρ., 1, p. 36, 15 Heib. διὸ οὐκ ἠξίουν αὐτὴν (sc. τὴν ἰητρικήν) ἔγωγε καινῆς ὑποθέσιος δεῖσθαι, ὥσπερ τὰ ἀφανέα τε καὶ ἀπορεόμενα, περὶ ὧν ἀνάγκη . . . ὑποθέσει χρῆσθαι, οἷον περὶ τῶν μετεώρων ἢ τῶν ὑπὸ γῆν.

[25] ⟨ἐπὶ τῶν⟩ τὴν ἐκ τῶν ἀποστημάτων φαντασίαν παραδιδόντων. The addition by Bignone, ⟨ἐπὶ τῶν⟩, has been adopted by Bailey.

[26] I here adopt von der Muehll's transposition of the words καὶ ἐν ποίοις ($B^1$ QCo: ἐφ' οἷοις $FP^3$ Z) ὁμοίως ἀταρακτῆσαι from the phrase which follows, 80, 10.

[27] Literally, 'as though it should exist for us', ὥσπερ οὖσαν κατ' αὐτούς, cf. *k.d.*, ii ὁ θάνατος οὐδὲν πρὸς ἡμᾶς, *Ep.*, III, 124, 7 μηδὲν πρὸς ἡμᾶς εἶναι τὸν θάνατον.

[28] ἰδιολογίας, a correction of H. Etienne from ἰδιαλογίας ($BP^1$ QCo), seems to me far superior to ἤδη ἀλογίας ($FHP^3$ Z) for carrying on the idea just before expressed by ἀξιώματα κενὰ καὶ νομοθεσίας. ἰδιολογέω can, it seems, be found in the same sense in Philodemus, *Acad. Ind.*, p. 4, Mekler.

[29] No doubt Bk. XI. Also, according to Epicurus the stars move in a straight line, cf. Theon, *Comm. sur l'Almageste*, p. 339, Rome.

[30] See also 102, 3-6 and 112, 6-8.

[31] αἱ δ' ἐπισημασίαι αἱ γιγνόμεναι ἐπί τισι ζῴοις κατὰ συγκύρημα γίνονται τοῦ καιροῦ, cf. 98, 9 ἐπισημασίαι δύνανται γίνεσθαι καὶ κατὰ συγκυρήσεις καιρῶν, καθάπερ ἐν τοῖς ἐμφανέσι παρ' ἡμῖν ζῴοις. Ernout translates ζῴοις (115, 9) by 'signs of the zodiac', and it is certain that the action of these signs on the weather later played an important part in Graeco-Roman astrology, cf. Ptol., *Tetrab.*, II, 12, p. 95ff. Boll-Boer, and Bouche-Leclerq, *L'Astrologie grecque*, p. 366. But, apart from the parallel indicated which favours the meaning 'animals', there is no question as far as I am aware of the zodiac in classical Greek meteorology. Aristotle, who is the first to speak of the ζῴδια does not mention them in that connection. Besides, ζῷον for ζῴδιον is a rare and late use, Ps. Man., II, 166, Herm. Tris., *Kore Kosm.*, 18 (p. 468, 6 Sc. τὰ ἀνθρωποειδῆ τῶν ζῴων.). Lastly, ἐξόδους cannot mean 'risings' and in any case will hardly suit the signs of the zodiac; they do not 'rise', it is the planets that 'rise' and by their passage through such-and-such a sign of the zodiac cause the effects on earth. It is much better then to keep the accepted translation (Bignone, Bailey); the animals by their goings and comings seem to foretell what the weather will be. This rustic form of prognostication was well known in Greece.

[32] ἀποτελεῖσθαι has no doubt an astrological ring, but not before the Roman epoch (ἀποτέλεσμα in Philodemus, 1st century B.C.). Here it has simply the classical meaning of 'happening' habitual in Plato, Aristotle, and Epicurus himself, cf. 104, 2 ἐνδέχεται κεραυνοὺς ἀποτελεῖσθαι.

[33] See also 115, 8 if we accept the correction ἄμυθοι (Lortzing) for ἀμύθητοι.

[34] The void, where the worlds and the gods have their being.

[35] How this idea became current in all the Schools and not only in Stoicism is proved by the Epicurean Diogenes of Oenoanda (2nd century A.D.), fr. 24, col. I Will. καθ' ἑκάστην μὲν γὰρ ἀποτομὴν τῆς γῆς ἄλλων ἄλλη πατρίς ἐστιν, κατὰ δὲ τὴν ὅλην περιοχὴν τοῦδε τοῦ κόσμου μία πάντων πατρίς ἐστιν ἡ πᾶσα γῆ, καὶ εἷς ὁ κόσμος οἶκος.

[36] Pyrrho, with his master Anaxarchus, took part in the expedition of Alexander. Cf. Diog. Laert., IX, 63 ἐκπατεῖν τ' αὐτὸν καὶ ἐρημάζειν, σπανίως ποτ' ἐπιφαινόμενον τοῖς οἴκοι· τοῦτο δὲ ποιεῖν ἀκούσαντα 'Ινδοῦ τινος ὀνειδίζοντος 'Αναξάρχῳ ὡς οὐκ ἂν ἕτερόν τινα διδάξαι οὗτος ἀγαθόν, αὐτὸς αὐλὰς βασιλικὰς θεραπεύων, and V. Brochard, *Les Sceptiques grecs*, 2nd edn. (Paris, 1923), pp. 73-5 and Edwyn Bevan, *Stoics and Sceptics* (Oxford, 1913), p. 123.

[37] Aristotles *ap.* Euseb., *Pr. ev.*, XIV, 18, 2-3 = Ritter and Preller, 8th edn., no. 446. Trad. Brochard (p. 54) slightly altered.

[38] Diog. Laert., IX, 107 = Ritter and Preller, no. 450.

[39] Sext. Emp., *Pyrrh. Hyp.*, I, 29 = Ritter and Preller no. 452. It is clear that οἷον τυχικῶς is an explanatory note by Sextus Empiricus. In fact, there is a close connection between scepticism and *ataraxia*, perhaps, in Pyrrho, with the distinction noted by Brochard (p. 67): 'His scepticism comes from his indifference rather than his indifference from his scepticism.' – Notice

(1) that in Diogenes Laertius and Sextus Empiricus the same image is repeated (σκιᾶς τρόπον D.L., ὡς σκιὰ σώματι S.E.);

(2) that this image, in Diogenes, is attributed to Timon, and this same Timon, in Aristocles and Diogenes, attests the Pyrrhonian origin of the doctrine of the connection between ἐποχή and ἀταραξία. This shows that the primary source, common to Aristocles, Diogenes Laertius, and Sextus Empiricus, is certainly Timon, an immediate disciple of Pyrrho, and so the doctrine of Pyrrhonian *ataraxia* is firmly established.

[40] Tim. *ap.* S. Emp., *Adv. eth.* (= *Adv. math.*, XI), 1 (= fr. 67 Diels, *Poetar. philosoph. fr.*, Berlin, 1901, pp. 173ff) ῥῆστα μεθ' ἡσυχίης | αἰεὶ ἀφροντίστως καὶ ἀκινήτως κατὰ ταὐτά, | μὴ προσέχων †δειλοῖς† ἡδυλόγου σοφίης (δειλοῖς corruptum: αἰνοῖς R. G. Bury [*Loeb. Cl. Lib.*, 1936, vol. III, p. 384], δίνοις Nauck; alii alia). Cf. Tim. *ap.* Diog. Laert., IX, 65 (*ib.*, Diels) πῶς ποτ' ἀνὴρ ἔτ' ἄγεις ῥῆστα μεθ' ἡσυχίης.

[41] Tim., *ap.* S. Emp., *Adv. eth.*, 141 (fr. 63-4 Diels) πάντῃ γὰρ ἐπεῖχε γαλήνη, *ib.* ἐν νηνεμίῃσι γαλήνης.

[42] Tim. *ap.* Diog. Laert., IX, 65 + Sext. Emp., *Adv. gramm.* (= *Adv. math.*, I), 305 = fr. 67 Diels.

[43] Diog. Laert., *Vita Epic.*, 10 καὶ χαλεπωτάτων δὲ καιρῶν κατασχόντων τηνικάδε τὴν 'Ελλάδα, and Menander, a direct witness, *Perikeirom.*, 282-5 πολλῶν γεγονότων ἀθλίων κατὰ τὸν χρόνον | τὸν νῦν – φορὰ γὰρ γέγονε τούτου νῦν καλή | ἐν ἅπασι τοῖς 'Ελλησι δι' ὅτι δή ποτε – | οὐδένα νομίζω κτλ.

[44] ἐξ ὧν ἰσότατος γίνεται ἀνδρὶ βίος, Tim. *ap.* S. Emp., *Adv. eth.*, 20 (= pr. 68 Diels).

[45] τέλος εἶναι τὴν ἀδιαφορίαν: Ariston, *SVF*, I, 83, 7.

[46] ὁ σοφὸς ὑπὸ τῆς τύχης ἀήττητός ἐστι καὶ ἀδούλωτος καὶ ἀκέραιος καὶ ἀπαθής Persaeus, *SVF*, I, 92, 22.

[47] *Unde Stoici* . . . τὴν ἀταραχίαν τῆς ψυχῆς, *hoc est nihil timere nec cupere, summum bonum esse*: Chrysippus, *SVF*, III, 109, 18.

[48] Cf. V. Brochard, *op. cit.*, pp. 60ff.

[49] ἦ γὰρ ἐγὼν ἐρέω ὥς μοι καταφαίνεται εἶναι | μῦθον ἀληθείης, ὀρθὸν ἔχων κανόνα, | ὡς ἡ τοῦ θείου τε φύσις καὶ τἀγαθοῦ ἔχει (Natorp: αἰει codd.), | ἐξ ὧν ἰσότατος γίνεται ἀνδρὶ βίος, Tim. *ap.* S. Emp., *Adv. eth.*, 20 (=fr. 68 Diels).

[50] μὴ προσέχων αἴνοις (?) ἡδυλόγου σοφίης, Tim. *ap.* S. Emp., Adv. eth., 1 (=fr. 68 Diels).

[51] Of the intellectual soul which comes from the Heavens and was given us by God as a δαίμων πάρεδρος. Cf. 90a 2 τὸ δὲ δὴ περὶ τοῦ κυριωτάτου παρ' ἡμῖν ψυχῆς εἴδους διανοεῖσθαι δεῖ τῇδε, ὡς ἄρα δαίμονα θεὸς ἑκάστῳ δέδωκεν. By virtue of this affinity with the Heavens the soul draws us upwards, ὡς ὄντας φυτὸν οὐκ ἔγγειον ἀλλὰ οὐράνιον (90a 7).

[52] J. U. Powell, *Collectanea Alexandrina* (Oxford, 1925), p. 229, no. 2.

[53] Antigonus Gonatas, Marcus Aurelius.

[54] Powell, p. 227, no. 1, v 7-8.

[55] εἰς τὸ πᾶν ἀεὶ ὁρᾶν, XII, 18.

# BIBLIOGRAPHY

THE *Epicurea* of Usener (1887) remains the indispensable source (for the fragments I have followed the numeration of Usener pp. 91ff). For the *Gnomologium Vaticanum*, cf. Usener, *Kl. Schr.*, I, pp. 297-325. I have also made use of the Italian translation (with notes) of E. Bignone (Bari, 1920) and especially of the edition (with English translation and commentary) by Cyril Bailey (Oxford, 1926).

On the personality of Epicurus himself, apart from the *Epicurea* cf. the Herculanean papyri 176, 1289 and 1232, published by A. Vogliano (*Epicuri et Epicureorum scripta in Herculanensibus papyris servata*, Berlin, 1928), pp. 23ff. (Epicureus incertus), 59-73 (Philod., π. Ἐπικούρου B and π. Ἐπικούρου), the letter to Idomeneus 'On Pride', published by Ch. Jensen, *Ein neuer Brief Epikurs* (*Abh. Göttingen*, Phil-Hist. Kl., III 5, Berlin, 1933), in particular pp. 75-83, and C. Diano, *Lettere di Epicuro e dei suoi*, Firenze, 1946; see also Usener's article (already mentioned) and H. V. Arnim, *P. W.*, VI, 133ff (1909).

On the ethical teaching of Epicurus, cf. W. Schmid, *Ethica Epicurea* (Pap. Herc. 1251), Leipzig, 1939; C. Diano, *Epicuri Ethica*, Firenze, 1946, and Id. ap. *Stud. it. di filol. class.*, XXIII, 1948, pp. 3ff.

On the religion and theology of Epicurus, apart from the *Epicurea* cf. Philodemus, π. εὐσεβείας (ed. Th. Gomperz, *Herculanische Studien*, II, Leipzig, 1866: on this work see especially R. Philippson, *Hermes*, LV, 1920, pp. 225ff. [1st book, 1st part; a review of the gods of mythology], 364ff. [1st book, 2nd part; a review of the δόξαι of the philosophers, cf. Cicero, N.D. I], LVI, 1921, pp. 355ff. [2nd book; an account of the religion of Epicurus]) and π. θεῶν,A,Γ (ed. H. Diels, *Abh. Berlin*, 1916-1917), and the letter (? of Epicurus) published by H. Diels, *Sitz. Ber. Berlin*, 1916 (XXXVII), pp. 886ff and Ch. Jensen, op. cit.; see also W. Scott, *J. of Phil.*, XII, pp. 212-47, R. Philippson, *Hermes*, LI (1916), pp. 568-608, LIII (1918), pp. 358-538, N. W. DeWitt, *The Gods of Epicurus and the Canon*, ap.

*Trans. Roy. Soc. of Canada*, Ottawa, XXXVI, 1942, pp. 33ff, W. Schmid, *Götter und Menschen in der Theologie Epikurs*, ap. *Rh. Mus.*, 1951, pp. 97ff, and F. Solmsen, *Epicurus and Cosmological Heresies*, ap. *Am. J. Phil.*, LXXII, 1951, pp. 1ff.

On Epicurus and Aristotle, cf. the work, already cited, of Bignone, *passim*.

It goes without saying that this bibliography does not pretend to be complete; I have deliberately left on one side everything concerning the Canonic and Physics of Epicurus. On this point cf. J. Haussleiter in the *Bursian* of 1937 (Nacharistotelische Philosophie, 1926-1930), pp. 13-18, and add the edition of the fragments of the π. φύσεως by A. Vogliano, *Rend. d. R. Acc. di Bologna, Cl. di scienze morali*, ser. III, vol. VI (1931-1932), pp. 33-76 and *Public. Soc. Fouad I de Papyrol., Textes et Documents*, IV, Cairo, 1940 (a fragment of Bk. XI). See also W. Schmid, *Epikurs Kritik der platonischen Elementarlehre*, Leipzig, 1936; Id., *Nugae Herculanenses*, ap. *Rh. Mus.*, 1943, pp. 35ff, N. W. DeWitt ap. *Cl. Phil.*, XXXI, 1936, pp. 206ff, *Trans. Amer. Phil. Ass.*, LXX, 1939, pp. 414ff, LXXIV, 1943, pp. 19ff; A. Barigazzi ap. *Stud. it. di filol. class.*, XXIII, 1948, pp. 179ff, XXIV, 1949, pp. 3ff.

On the portraits of Epicurus cf. K. S. Schefold, *Die Bildnisse d. antiken Dichter*, etc., Basel, 1943, pp. 38ff, 116ff, and F. Poulsen ap. *Acta Archaeol.*, XVI, 1945, pp. 178ff.

Finally, I must mention an important review of my little book (French edition) by N. W. DeWitt in *Am. J. Phil.*, LXVIII, 1947, pp. 317ff.

## A LIST OF ABBREVIATIONS USED MAINLY IN THE NOTES

*Abh. Berlin* — Abhandlungen der preuss. Akademie der Wissenschaften (Berlin)
*Arch. Gesch. Phil.* — Archiv für Geschischte der Philosophie
*ARW* — Archiv für Religionswissenschaften
*BCH* — Bulletin de Correspondance Hellenique
*CIG* — Corpus Inscriptionum Graecarum
*CRAI* — Comptes rendus de l'Académie des Inscriptions et Belles-Lettres
Diels-Kranz — Fragmente der Vorsokratiker (5th edn.)
Firm. Mat. — Firmicus Maternus (De errore profanarum religionum)
*Gn. V.* — Gnomologium Vaticanum.
*Inscr. gr. l. Syrie* — Inscriptions grecques et latines de la Syrie
*Jahrb. f. class. Phil.* — Jahrbücher für klassische Philologie (ed. A. Körte)
*k.d.* — κύριαι δόξαι = Principal Doctrines
*L. S. J.* — Liddell-Scott-Jones, A Greek English Lexicon
*MAMA* — Monumenta Asiae Minoris Antiqua
Michel — Recueil d'inscriptions grecques ed. C. Michel
*OGI* — Orientis Graeci Inscriptiones Selectae (ed. Dittenberger)
*P. W.* — Pauly-Wissowa Real-Encyclopädie der klassischen Altertumwissenschaft
*Ps.Man.* — Pseudo-Manetho
*Rech. Sc. Relig.* — Recherches de science religieuse
*REG* — Revue des Études grecques
*RGVV* — Religionsgeschichtliche Versuche und Vorarbeiten
*Rh. Mus.* — Rheinisches Museum
*SEG* — Supplementum Epigraphicum Graecum
*SIG* — Sylloge Inscriptionum Graecarum ed. Dittenberger (3rd edn.)
*Sitz. Ber. Berlin* — Sitzungsberichte der kgl. preuss. Akademie der Wissenschaften (Berlin)
*SVF* — Stoicorum Veterorum Fragmenta ed. von Arnim
v.g. — verbi gratia

The following books by the same author are also referred to by abbreviated titles:

L'Idéal religieux des Grecs et l'Evangile (Paris, 1932)
Le Monde gréco-romain au temps de Notre Seigneur (Paris, 1935)
Contemplation et Vie contemplative selon Platon (Paris, 1936)
La Sainteté (Paris, 1942)

## INDEX

www.ingramcontent.com/pod-product-compliance
Lightning Source LLC
LaVergne TN
LVHW020644100826
845148LV00012B/2328

* 9 7 8 1 5 9 7 4 0 6 5 6 7 *